Unraveling the Storm: A Chaotic Dance of Climate and Conflict

Collier Deborah Maria

Published by Collier Deborah Maria, 2024.

While every precaution has been taken in the preparation of this book, the publisher assumes no responsibility for errors or omissions, or for damages resulting from the use of the information contained herein.

UNRAVELING THE STORM: A CHAOTIC DANCE OF CLIMATE AND CONFLICT

First edition. March 15, 2024.

ISBN: 979-8224996346

Written by Collier Deborah Maria.

Table of Contents

Introduction. Understanding Climate Change and Conflict: An Overview

Climate change is a pressing global issue that has become a significant concern in recent years. The effects of rising global temperatures, changing weather patterns, and extreme weather events have dire consequences for both people and the environment. One of the lesser-known impacts of climate change is its potential to increase the risk of conflicts and exacerbate existing tensions.

Understanding the relationship between climate change and conflict is crucial for policymakers, researchers, and communities alike. This overview aims to provide a comprehensive understanding of the complex interactions between climate change and conflict, highlighting the key factors, mechanisms, and consequences involved.

The recognition of climate change as a driver of conflict has gained increasing attention over the past two decades. The Intergovernmental Panel on Climate Change (IPCC) and other scientific bodies have established a clear link between anthropogenic greenhouse gas emissions and rising global temperatures. As a result, we are witnessing more frequent and intense heatwaves, droughts, floods, and storms, leading to adverse impacts on water and food security, displacement, and resource competition.

These climate-related impacts can escalate tensions, particularly in regions already affected by political instability, economic grievances, or identity conflicts. Scarce resources, such as water, fertile land, or valuable natural resources, can become contentious issues, further fueling existing conflicts or acting as triggers for new ones. In some cases, climate change-induced disasters can directly contribute to the outbreak of conflicts as communities compete for limited resources or are forced to migrate, leading to strained relations or even violence.

Understanding the mechanisms through which climate change interacts with conflict is essential for effective risk assessment and conflict prevention interventions. Climate change can exacerbate existing political, social, and economic vulnerabilities within a society. For example, in areas heavily dependent on agriculture, climate-induced crop failures can lead to food shortages and increase economic disparities, significantly impacting vulnerable populations.

Furthermore, climate change indirectly affects conflict dynamics through its impact on key sectors such as agriculture, fisheries, or tourism, which are critical for people's livelihoods. Disruptions to these sectors can lead to job losses, economic downturns, and social unrest, creating a fertile ground for conflicts to arise.

Moreover, climate change influences the behavior of non-state armed groups, terrorist organizations, or insurgent movements. Groups looking to exploit social tensions or vulnerable communities may find opportunities in areas affected by climate-related disasters. They can offer immediate relief or engage in illegal activities, further worsening the situation and, in some cases, directly contributing to conflicts.

The consequences of climate change-induced conflicts are far-reaching, impacting both human lives and the environment. Climate-related conflicts can result in large-scale displacement, loss of lives and livelihoods, deteriorating social cohesion, and weakened institutions. Additionally, conflicts can have long-term environmental consequences, such as deforestation, soil erosion, or damage to ecosystems, further exacerbating climate change and perpetuating a vicious cycle.

Recognizing the complexity and multifaceted nature of the climate change-conflict relationship is crucial for developing effective strategies to mitigate and manage its potential impacts. This overview aims to provide a foundation for further research, policy development, and action to address the interconnected challenges of climate change and conflict.

In the following sections, we will delve into the various dimensions of the climate change-conflict nexus, exploring case studies, theories, and empirical evidence that shed light on this critically important topic. By gaining a comprehensive understanding of these dynamics, we can work towards minimizing the risk of conflicts spurred by climate change and promoting peaceful coexistence in a changing world.

Chapter 1: Climate Change and Resource Scarcity

In recent decades, climate change and resource scarcity have emerged as the most pressing challenges facing the planet. As the global population continues to grow and industrialization spreads, the demand for resources like water, energy, and land has skyrocketed. At the same time, human activities have unleashed significant greenhouse gas emissions, leading to unprecedented changes in the Earth's climate system. This chapter will delve into the central issues of climate change and resource scarcity, exploring their interconnections and consequences for the future of our planet.

Climate Change:

Climate change refers to long-term alterations in temperature patterns, precipitation amounts, wind patterns, and other aspects of weather on Earth. The primary driver of these changes is the increase in greenhouse gases, such as carbon dioxide (CO_2), in the atmosphere. While these gases are essential for maintaining Earth's temperature, excessive emissions disrupt the delicate balance and lead to a buildup of heat-trapping gases. This phenomenon, commonly referred to as global warming, has far-reaching implications.

Impacts of Climate Change:

The impacts of climate change are varied and widespread. Rising global temperatures have caused the melting of polar ice caps and glaciers, resulting in rising sea levels and increased frequency and intensity of natural disasters like hurricanes and storms. Heatwaves have become more frequent, posing risks to human health and agriculture. Changing rainfall patterns have disrupted ecosystems, leading to more frequent droughts and floods, affecting food production and water supply. Biodiversity loss and the spread of infectious diseases are other notable consequences of climate change. These impacts have severe social, economic, and environmental consequences.

Link to Resource Scarcity:

Climate change exacerbates resource scarcity, creating a vicious cycle of interrelated challenges. For instance, as precipitation patterns shift, certain regions may experience droughts, reducing water availability for agriculture, drinking water, and other essential needs. This, in turn, can cause food shortages and price hikes, disproportionately affecting vulnerable communities. Additionally, the rising sea levels and increased frequency of extreme weather events can intensify competition for scarce resources like land, exacerbating conflicts and displacements.

Energy and Fossil Fuels:

One of the main contributors to climate change is the burning of fossil fuels for energy generation. Fossil fuels, such as coal, oil, and natural gas, release substantial amounts of CO_2 into the atmosphere when burned. As nations seek to meet their growing energy demands, finding sustainable alternatives to fossil fuels becomes imperative. Transitioning to renewable energy sources like solar, wind, and hydroelectric power can help mitigate climate change and alleviate resource scarcity.

Water Scarcity:

Water scarcity is another critical issue closely linked to climate change. As temperature and evaporation rates increase, freshwater availability diminishes. This scarcity can lead to conflicts over water resources, especially in regions heavily reliant on agriculture. Addressing water scarcity requires innovative approaches such as water reclamation, rainwater harvesting, and improving water-use efficiency in various industries.

IN CHAPTER 1, WE EXPLORED the intricate relationship between climate change and resource scarcity. We witnessed how climate change amplifies resource scarcity and jeopardizes the stability of crucial elements like water and energy. To combat these challenges, policymakers, businesses, and individuals must adopt sustainable practices and prioritize the transition to renewable energy sources. Only through concerted efforts and united approach can we ensure the preservation of essential resources, mitigate climate change, and create a sustainable future for generations to come.

1.1 Potential Impacts on Water Resources

One of the potential impacts on water resources is the increased demand for water due to population growth. As the world population continues to grow rapidly, the demand for clean and safe drinking water is also rising. This puts pressure on existing water sources and can lead to over-extraction of water from aquifers and rivers.

Moreover, climate change is another factor that can have significant impacts on water resources. With changing weather patterns, some regions may experience increased water scarcity due to prolonged droughts, while others may face more intense and frequent rainfall, leading to increased risks of flooding. These extreme weather events can disrupt the water cycle and affect the availability and quality of water.

Additionally, human activities like industrialization and agriculture have a major impact on water resources. Industrial processes often generate pollution that can contaminate water bodies, making them unfit for human consumption or harming aquatic ecosystems. Similarly, agricultural activities require large amounts of water for irrigation, and inefficient irrigation techniques can lead to water wastage and depletion of water sources.

Furthermore, deforestation and land-use changes can also impact water resources. Trees play a crucial role in maintaining the water cycle by absorbing water from the ground and releasing it into the atmosphere through evapotranspiration. When forests are cleared for agriculture or urbanization, the water-holding capacity of the land decreases, leading to increased runoff and reduced groundwater recharge.

The potential impacts on water resources also include the pollution caused by improper waste management. Improper disposal of waste, particularly hazardous substances, can contaminate water bodies and have severe consequences for human health and the environment. Industrial waste, agricultural runoff, and untreated sewage are major contributors to water pollution, compromising the quality of available water sources.

Lastly, the over-extraction of groundwater for domestic, industrial, and agricultural purposes can lead to the depletion of aquifers. In many regions, groundwater reserves are being pumped at unsustainable rates, leading to the lowering of water tables. If this over-extraction continues, it can result in long-term water scarcity and irreversible damage to ecosystems that depend on groundwater.

In conclusion, the potential impacts on water resources are diverse and interconnected. Factors such as population growth, climate change, human activities, deforestation, pollution, and over-extraction of groundwater all play a role in shaping the present and future status of our water resources. It is crucial to implement sustainable water management practices to mitigate these impacts and ensure the availability of clean water for current and future generations.

1.2 Implications for Food Security

Food security refers to the availability and access to sufficient, safe, and nutritious food that meets the dietary needs and preferences of individuals. It also includes the ability to acquire food in a sustainable and dignified manner. There are several direct and indirect implications for food security as a result of various factors that affect the food system.

One implication for food security is the impact of climate change. The changing climate patterns, such as increasing temperatures, erratic rainfall, and extreme weather events, pose significant risks to agricultural production. These changes can negatively affect crop yields, water availability, and livestock production. For regions that heavily rely on agriculture for food, income, and employment, these climate-related factors can disrupt food production, leading to decreased availability and increased prices of food. Vulnerable populations may struggle to access the necessary nutritious food, leading to food insecurity and malnutrition.

Another implication for food security is the issue of food waste and loss. According to the Food and Agriculture Organization (FAO), approximately one-third of all food produced globally is either lost or wasted. This includes food lost in production, storage, transportation, and consumption. Food waste not only represents a significant waste of resources but also has implications for food security. The resources invested in producing and distributing food that goes to waste could have been used to feed more people. Additionally, food waste generates greenhouse gas emissions, contributing to climate change. Reducing food waste and loss is crucial to improving food security as it ensures that available food reaches those who need it the most.

Global economic inequalities also have implications for food security. In developing countries, poverty levels are often high, and securing food becomes a daily struggle for many households. Limited access to resources, such as land, water, seeds, and fertilizers, can hinder small-scale farmers from improving their productivity and overall food security. Inadequate infrastructure and limited market access also limit their ability to sell their produce at fair prices, perpetuating poverty and food insecurity. Addressing economic disparities and empowering vulnerable communities is essential to achieving food security goals.

The globalization of the food system has further implications for food security. As food production and distribution become more integrated on a global scale, the reliance on a few key crops and varieties increases. Dependence on a limited range of crops for food can be risky, particularly in the face of climate change and emerging diseases or pests. If a major staple crop is affected by a disease outbreak or severe weather event, it can have severe implications for food security. Diversifying agricultural systems, promoting sustainable farming practices, and supporting local food production can help reduce these risks and increase resilience to potential shocks.

In conclusion, there are numerous implications for food security, ranging from climate change and its impact on agricultural productivity to food waste and loss, economic inequalities, and the globalization of the food system. Addressing these challenges requires a comprehensive approach that involves sustainable and resilient agricultural practices, reducing food waste, promoting equitable access to resources, and empowering vulnerable communities. Only through concerted efforts and collaboration can we effectively tackle the complexities of food security and ensure that everyone has access to safe and nutritious food.

1.3 Impact on Energy Sources

The impact of energy sources on various aspects of our lives is an important and crucial issue that needs to be thoroughly understood and analyzed. Energy sources play a crucial role in powering different sectors of the economy, such as transportation, industrial operations, and residential usage. However, as the world progresses and technologies evolve, there is an increasing need to explore and adopt cleaner and more sustainable energy sources. In this article, we will delve into the impact of energy sources on various aspects and the consequences of our choices.

One key aspect to evaluate is the environmental impact of different energy sources. Fossil fuel-based sources such as coal, oil, and natural gas have been the primary sources of energy for many decades. However, they have posed significant threats to the environment, contributing to air pollution and greenhouse gas emissions. The combustion of these fossil fuels releases carbon dioxide and other harmful pollutants into the atmosphere, leading to climate change and adverse health effects. It is essential to acknowledge the detrimental impact of fossil fuels and consider alternative energy sources to mitigate these issues.

Renewable energy sources offer a promising and sustainable solution. Solar energy, wind power, hydropower, geothermal energy, and biomass represent renewable energy resources that have shown tremendous potential in recent years. Solar energy captures the power of the sun and converts it into electricity, which can be utilized for various purposes. Wind power harnesses the kinetic energy of wind and converts it into electricity through turbines. Hydropower utilizes the force of water to produce electricity, while geothermal energy taps into the Earth's heat to generate power. Biomass involves extracting energy from organic materials such as plants and agricultural waste. These renewable energy sources offer significant advantages by reducing greenhouse gas emissions and increasing energy efficiency, ultimately leading to a cleaner and greener environment.

Another crucial factor to consider is the impact of energy sources on energy security. Fossil fuels, being finite resources, are subject to geopolitical tensions and price fluctuations. Countries heavily reliant on imported fossil fuels may face energy insecurities, comprising high costs, market volatility, and potential conflicts over access to resources. On the other hand, by embracing renewable energy sources and working towards energy independence, nations can become less dependent on external sources of energy and enhance their energy security. Additionally, renewable energy technologies can be deployed across a diverse range of locations, reducing the vulnerability associated with centralized energy infrastructures.

Furthermore, renewable energy sources offer economic benefits. As countries transition towards renewable energy, they are investing in technology development, infrastructure, and the creation of a sustainable energy market. This presents significant opportunities for job creation, particularly in the renewable energy industry. The clean energy sector has already been generating new employment opportunities, with roles ranging from manufacturing and installation to operation and maintenance of renewable energy systems. In addition, the deployment of renewable energy technologies can also stimulate local economies and provide support for rural communities.

The impact of energy sources extends beyond environmental and economic aspects to societal and health-related issues. The undesirable consequences of fossil fuel combustion on human health are well-documented, with air pollution causing respiratory diseases and other health issues. By transitioning to cleaner energy sources, we can mitigate these health risks and improve public well-being significantly. Additionally, renewable energy projects often involve community engagement and provide greater opportunities for public participation, allowing for a more inclusive and sustainable approach to energy development.

In conclusion, energy sources have a profound impact on various aspects of our lives. Though fossil fuels have been dominant for a long time, it is becoming increasingly evident that they are not sustainable or environmentally friendly choices. By embracing and expanding the use of renewable energy sources, we can address environmental concerns, enhance energy security, stimulate economic growth, and protect public health. The transition to clean and sustainable energy sources is not only a necessity but also an opportunity for a better and more prosperous future.

UNRAVELING THE STORM: A CHAOTIC DANCE OF CLIMATE AND CONFLICT

economic growth, and protect public health. The transition to clean and sustainable energy sources is not only a necessity but also an opportunity for a better and more prosperous future.

Chapter 2: Displacement and Climate Change

Displacement caused by climate change is an urgent and pressing issue that affects millions of people around the world. As the Earth's climate continues to change and temperatures rise, the frequency and intensity of extreme weather events such as hurricanes, droughts, floods, and heatwaves are increasing. These events are forcing countless individuals and communities to flee their homes in search of safety and refuge. In this chapter, we will delve into the complexities of displacement caused by climate change, examining the underlying factors, the range of impacts, and potential solutions to address this profound challenge.

Understanding Displacement:

Displacement, as it pertains to climate change, refers to the enforced movement of individuals or communities from their homes and habitual living spaces due to the impacts of climate-related events. This can occur both within countries (internal displacement) and across international borders (cross-border displacement). The causes of displacement are multifaceted, influenced by a combination of environmental, social, economic, and political factors. Displacement can be sudden and acute, such as in the aftermath of a devastating hurricane, or it can be gradual, as changing weather patterns erode livelihoods and increase vulnerability over time.

Impacts of Displacement:

The impacts of displacement caused by climate change are far-reaching and profound. First and foremost, human lives are put at risk as individuals are forced to flee their homes in situations of extreme danger. Displaced populations often endure inadequate living conditions, lack of access to essential services such as clean water and healthcare, and face increased exposure to diseases and other health risks. Displacement also disrupts social fabrics, leads to the breakdown of communities and social networks, and exacerbates existing inequalities. Additionally, the loss of homes and means of livelihood diminishes economic opportunities, pushing displaced populations into a cycle of poverty and dependency.

Key Drivers of Displacement:

Several key drivers contribute to the displacement caused by climate change. These include the increasingly frequent and intense extreme weather events mentioned earlier. For example, rising sea levels resulting from climate change threaten coastal communities, making them more susceptible to storm surges and flooding. Shifts in precipitation patterns and prolonged droughts also contribute to rural-to-urban migration as agricultural livelihoods become unstable. Additionally, the eroding coastline and vanishing freshwater sources displace indigenous communities who have traditionally relied on these natural resources for their sustenance and cultural practices.

Mitigation and Adaptation Strategies:

Addressing displacement caused by climate change necessitates a comprehensive and multifaceted approach. At the global level, there is an urgent need for concerted action to reduce greenhouse gas emissions and limit global warming. Mitigation strategies such as transitioning to renewable energy sources, promoting sustainable land and water management practices, and adopting more climate-resilient infrastructure can all help reduce the frequency and intensity of climate-related events, thus mitigating the displacement they cause. However, as we currently face the impacts of climate change, adaptation strategies are equally essential. These involve supporting communities in building resilience through measures such as early warning systems, disaster risk reduction programs, robust social safety nets, and relocation when necessary, ensuring the rights and dignity of displaced individuals are upheld.

DISPLACEMENT CAUSED by climate change presents one of the most daunting challenges of our time. As the impacts of climate change continue to unfold, the number of individuals forced to leave their homes and communities will only increase, potentially leading to conflicts, instability, and widespread human suffering. Recognizing the multidimensional nature of the issue, it is imperative for governments, international organizations, and civil society to collaborate and develop innovative solutions to address this crisis. By investing in both mitigation and adaptation strategies, we can work towards a more sustainable and resilient future, where displacement caused by climate change is minimized, and the rights and dignity of all individuals are protected.

2.1 Climate-induced Migration Patterns

Climate-induced migration refers to the movement of people from one place to another as a result of the impact of climate change on their communities. This type of migration is a complex phenomenon that is influenced by a variety of factors, including temperature, precipitation patterns, sea level rise, and extreme weather events.

One of the key patterns of climate-induced migration is the movement of people from rural areas to urban centers. Changing weather conditions and environmental degradation, such as drought, desertification, and reduced agricultural productivity, often make it difficult for rural communities to sustain their livelihoods and meet their basic needs. As a result, many people are forced to leave their homes in search of better economic opportunities and living conditions in urban areas. This often leads to rapid urbanization and the growth of informal settlements and slums in cities, which can put a strain on existing infrastructure and services.

Another migration pattern that is emerging as a result of climate change is the movement of people within and across borders due to the increasing frequency and intensity of extreme weather events. Events such as hurricanes, floods, and wildfires have the potential to destroy homes, infrastructure, and livelihoods, forcing people to seek refuge in safer areas. In some cases, these movements may be temporary, as people return to their homes once the immediate danger has passed. However, in other cases, these movements can lead to long-term displacement, as communities are unable to rebuild and recover from the impact of the disaster.

In addition to these patterns, climate-induced migration is also influenced by social, economic, and political factors. For example, poverty, inequality, and lack of access to resources and opportunities can exacerbate the vulnerability of communities to climate change and contribute to migration. Political instability, conflicts, and governance failures can also play a role in shaping migration patterns, as they can disrupt communities and make it difficult for people to live safely and securely in their homes.

It is worth noting that climate-induced migration is a complex and multi-dimensional issue that can have both positive and negative consequences. On the one hand, migration can offer opportunities for economic growth, cultural exchange, and social development. It can also provide a means of adapting to the impacts of climate change, as people move to areas that are less affected by extreme weather events. On the other hand, migration can also be a source of social and economic inequality, as marginalized groups may be disproportionately affected and excluded from the benefits of migration.

In conclusion, climate-induced migration is a significant and growing phenomenon that is shaped by a range of environmental, social, economic, and political factors. Understanding these patterns and their consequences is crucial for devising effective policies and strategies to mitigate the impacts of climate change and support the communities and individuals who are most affected.

2.2 Challenges in Refugee Protection

Refugee protection is a complex and multifaceted task that poses numerous challenges to governments, humanitarian organizations, and communities around the world. While the specific challenges may vary based on geographical location and political context, there are several overarching issues that recur in almost every situation. In this article, we will explore some of the key challenges in refugee protection, focusing on five main areas: legal and administrative complexities, resource constraints, protracted displacement, social integration, and vulnerability to abuse.

1. Legal and Administrative Complexities:

One significant challenge in refugee protection is the intricate web of legal and administrative systems that govern the process. Different jurisdictions may have varying definitions and criteria for refugee status determination, making it difficult for refugees to navigate and leaving them vulnerable to exploitation. Asylum procedures can be lengthy and arduous, often placing significant strain on both refugees and the organizations tasked with assisting them. Additionally, ensuring access to legal representation and effective remedies remains a challenge, particularly in situations where resources are limited.

2. Resource Constraints:

Addressing the needs of refugees requires significant resources, including financial assistance, healthcare, education, shelter, and basic necessities. However, resource constraints often make it challenging for host countries, civil society organizations, and humanitarian actors to adequately meet these demands. Limited funding and competing priorities can lead to inadequate service provision, resulting in dire living conditions and limited access to essential services. Insufficient resources also hinder the capacity-building efforts necessary for sustainable solutions, creating a cycle of dependence for both refugees and host communities.

3. Protracted Displacement:

Refugee situations are increasingly becoming protracted, meaning that refugees spend not months, but years in exile. This protracted displacement presents a considerable challenge as it makes finding durable solutions more challenging. Some refugees may be unable to return to their home countries due to continued conflict or persecution, while others may face difficulties in integrating into the host society. The prolongation of displacement exacerbates issues such as limited resources, decreased employment opportunities, and strained social and political dynamics, leading to the marginalization and vulnerability of displaced populations.

4. Social Integration:

The process of integrating refugees into host communities is a complex undertaking wrought with challenges. Language barriers, cultural differences, and prejudice can hinder social cohesion and create difficulties for the successful integration of refugees. Lack of social support networks can contribute to feelings of isolation and exclusion, impacting mental health and overall well-being. Host communities may also face resentment, xenophobia, and resource competition, further complicating integration efforts. It is essential to address these challenges through inclusive policies, community awareness campaigns, and programs that foster dialogue and mutual understanding.

5. Vulnerability to Abuse:

Refugees, especially women and children, are particularly vulnerable to various forms of abuse and exploitation. Trafficking, sexual and gender-based violence, child labor, and recruitment into armed conflict are some of the grave challenges that refugees face. Inadequate protection mechanisms, limited access to justice, and reduced functionality of legal frameworks in host countries exacerbate these vulnerabilities. Comprehensive protection measures, including effective screening processes, safe and supportive environments, and access to justice, are crucial in combating such abuses and ensuring the safety and dignity of refugees.

In conclusion, refugee protection is an intricate and challenging task that demands significant efforts and resources. Addressing the legal complexities, resource constraints, protracted displacement, social integration difficulties, and vulnerabilities to abuse are crucial for ensuring the effective protection and well-being of refugees. Collaborative efforts, involving governments, international organizations, civil society, and individuals, are essential in overcoming these challenges and upholding the rights and dignity of refugees worldwide.

2.3 Future Scenarios for Climate Displacement

Climate displacement refers to the phenomenon where individuals and communities are forced to flee their homes and lands due to the impacts of climate change. These include rising sea levels, extreme weather events, and prolonged droughts. As climate change accelerates, the future scenarios for climate displacement are becoming a growing concern. In this article, I will explore three future scenarios that might arise due to climate displacement.

1. Mass Migration: One possible future scenario is the mass migration of large populations from regions severely affected by climate change to relatively stable areas. This scenario could occur due to a combination of factors such as sea-level rise, desertification, and extreme weather events.

Coastal regions, especially low-lying island nations, are particularly vulnerable to rising sea levels. As these areas become uninhabitable, millions of people could be displaced and forced to move inland or seek refuge in other countries. This could lead to significant social and political challenges, as host countries might struggle to accommodate the influx of climate migrants.

In addition, regions experiencing prolonged droughts or extreme weather events, such as hurricanes and cyclones, could also witness mass migration. A lack of access to food, water, and basic amenities could push people to leave their homes and search for better living conditions elsewhere.

2. Environmental Refugees: Another possible future scenario is the emergence of a new category of refugees known as "environmental refugees." These individuals are forced to relocate due to the degradation and loss of their natural environment caused by climate change.

For example, communities dependent on agriculture or fishing for their livelihoods may face displacement due to severe changes in local ecosystems.

UNRAVELING THE STORM: A CHAOTIC DANCE OF CLIMATE AND CONFLICT

With rising temperatures and changing rainfall patterns, traditional farming practices may become unsustainable, leading to a loss of income and food security. Similarly, coastal communities reliant on fishing may witness the depletion of fish stocks and the destruction of coral reefs, forcing them to abandon their traditional way of life.

These environmental refugees may struggle to find new homes and livelihoods, leading to social unrest and heightened vulnerability. The international community will need to address the unique challenges posed by environmental refugees and develop strategies to support their needs.

3. Competition for Resources: The third future scenario for climate displacement is increased competition for resources, which could trigger conflicts and displacement. As climate change intensifies, access to freshwater, arable land, and other essential resources may become limited in certain regions.

Competition for resources could occur at various scales, ranging from local disputes between neighboring communities to large-scale conflicts between countries. For instance, areas suffering from water scarcity or reduced agricultural productivity may experience heightened tensions as communities fight over limited resources.

In some cases, existing social or political tensions may be exacerbated by climate change, leading to violence and forced displacement. The scarcity of resources could further exacerbate inequalities and deepen existing conflicts.

To mitigate the challenges posed by increased competition for resources, it is crucial for governments and communities to adopt sustainable practices, implement policies that promote resource sharing, and invest in alternative technologies that reduce reliance on scarce resources.

In conclusion, the future scenarios for climate displacement are multifaceted and pose significant challenges to individuals, communities, and countries. Mass migration, the emergence of environmental refugees, and increased competition for resources all represent possible outcomes of climate change. It is imperative for policymakers, organizations, and individuals to work together to address these challenges, develop equitable strategies, and ensure the well-being of those affected by climate displacement.

Chapter 3: Geopolitical Tensions and Climate Change

Geopolitical tensions have been a constant feature of international relations throughout history. War, conflicts, and political disputes have always shaped the global landscape. However, climate change has emerged as a significant factor that intensifies these geopolitical tensions. The impact of climate change on countries, resources, and migration patterns has created new challenges and amplified existing disputes, leading to heightened geopolitical rivalry. This chapter delves into the intricate relationship between climate change and geopolitical tensions, exploring the different dimensions, causes, and potential consequences.

1. Geopolitical Flashpoints:

Climate change has become a factor in several geopolitical flashpoints worldwide. From the Arctic to the South China Sea, countries are increasingly vying for control over resources and routes impacted by climate change. The melting Arctic ice has opened up new shipping routes and access to untapped reserves of natural resources, triggering territorial disputes among states bordering the region. The South China Sea, a vital maritime route, has witnessed evocative territorial claims, largely driven by the desire to control fossil fuel resources. These territorial disputes have the potential to escalate regional tensions and fuel conflicts.

2. Resource Scarcity:

Climate change-induced resource scarcity is a source of geopolitical tension. Rising temperatures, extreme weather events, and sea-level rise pose significant threats to agriculture, water availability, and energy resources in many regions. As these resources become scarcer, competition intensifies, leading to potential conflicts. Scarce water resources in the Middle East have been a recurring cause of tensions and can further destabilize the region. Similarly, competition over access to energy resources required for economic growth further exacerbates geopolitical rivalries.

3. Forced Migration and Refugees:

Climate change has led to increased forced migration and refugee flows, triggering geopolitical tensions. Rising sea levels and the loss of habitable land have displaced people, leading to the creation of climate change refugees. This has prompted border disputes as countries struggle to deal with mass migration. The migration crisis in Europe in recent years, driven in part by climate change-induced crises, has strain ERD relations among the affected countries and intensified geopolitical tensions within the European Union.

4. Geoengineering and Technological Advances:

Geoengineering, the large-scale manipulation of the Earth's climate systems, holds the potential to exacerbate geopolitical tensions. As countries explore geoengineering techniques to mitigate or counteract the effects of climate change, concerns about unintended consequences and inequalities arise. Developing and deploying these technologies on a global scale could create power imbalances and escalate conflicts over control and access to climate-altering technologies.

5. Climate Politics and Diplomacy:

Climate change influences geopolitical tensions by shaping international diplomatic relations and global politics. The Paris Agreement, an international commitment to combat climate change, has prompted cooperation and competition among nations. This voluntary agreement has become a platform for geopolitical rivalries, with certain countries trying to gain economic advantages by manipulating climate goals and international regulations. The power play between nations in climate negotiations can amplify geopolitical tensions and undermine collective action to combat climate change.

CLIMATE CHANGE HAS become a defining factor in geopolitical tensions around the world. Power struggles over resources, competition for control, forced migration, and climate policies all contribute to an intricate web of geopolitical rivalries. As nations grapple with the consequences of a changing climate, it is crucial to recognize and address the potential for geopolitical tensions to escalate. International cooperation, diplomatic solutions, and equitable distribution of resources can help mitigate these tensions and foster a sustainable global order that addresses the challenges posed by climate change.

3.1 Climate Change as a
Security Threat

Climate change is commonly recognized as one of the most pressing issues of our time, and its impacts are far-reaching and multi-dimensional. One aspect that deserves considerable attention is the notion of climate change as a security threat.

The security implications of climate change stem from its potential to exacerbate existing conflicts, create new sources of competition, and disrupt social and economic systems. These consequences are not mere hypothetical scenarios; they are already being witnessed in various parts of the world.

One area where climate change is fueling conflict is in regions already marred by political instability and resource scarcity. For example, in many arid and semi-arid regions of Africa, diminished rainfall and increased temperature are leading to a decline in agricultural productivity and water availability. These changes place added stress on already scarce resources, intensifying competition among communities and potentially triggering conflicts over land, water, and other essential commodities.

Similarly, the melting of polar ice caps has driven new territorial disputes in the Arctic. As ice recedes and opens up new shipping routes, countries vie for control over these navigable waterways as well as the vast untapped reserves of oil and gas underneath the changing ice. This scramble for resources not only raises geopolitical tensions but also increases the risk of conflicts in a previously stable region.

Moreover, climate change-induced migration poses security challenges for both sending and receiving countries. As extreme weather events become more frequent and intense, the number of people displaced by disasters is likely to rise. This displacement can disrupt social structures, strain resources, and heighten the potential for social unrest and conflict. Additionally, the arrival of large numbers of displaced people in host countries can further fuel existing tensions and potentially lead to political instability.

While it is evident that climate change has the potential to escalate conflicts, it is worth noting that it also strains states' capacities to respond to security threats. Governments worldwide face increasing demands on their resources due to the need for disaster management, rehabilitation, and adaptation measures. This diversion of resources impacts their ability to tackle other security challenges such as terrorism and regional conflicts. In this way, climate change acts as a threat multiplier by worsening existing security concerns and leaving countries vulnerable to new ones.

Recognizing climate change as a security threat is crucial for effective policymaking and international cooperation. Governments must integrate climate considerations into their security strategies, working to reduce vulnerability, address the root causes of conflicts arising from climate change, and promote sustainable and resilient development. Collaboration through agreements like the Paris Agreement is vital to adequately respond to the changing global security landscape and build more resilient and secure societies.

In conclusion, climate change presents a multifaceted security threat with far-reaching implications. The shifts in resource availability, increased competition, and climate-induced migration contribute to conflict and exacerbate existing security challenges. The long-term consequences of climate change necessitate a proactive approach, with governments recognizing the importance of integrating climate concerns into their security strategies. Only through global collaboration and concerted efforts can we effectively navigate the security risks posed by climate change.

3.2 Competition over Access to Natural Resources

Competition over access to natural resources is a longstanding and recurring issue in the world. Resources such as oil, gas, minerals, water, and land have become increasingly valuable as populations grow and economies develop. This competition often takes place on multiple levels, involving both national and international actors.

One of the key drivers of competition over natural resources is the growing demand for them. As countries become more industrialized and their populations increase, the demand for resources also rises. This creates the conditions for competition, as multiple actors seek to secure access to limited resources in order to meet their own needs and maintain their economic growth.

The competition for natural resources is not limited to one region or one type of resource. It occurs globally, affecting both developed and developing nations. For example, the quest for oil and gas reserves in the Middle East has been a focal point of international competition for decades. Similarly, the race to secure access to minerals essential for technological devices has intensified in recent years.

At a national level, competition over access to natural resources often leads to conflicts and disputes. In some cases, these conflicts can escalate into violence and even war. Several African countries, for instance, have experienced armed conflicts fueled by competition over mineral resources such as coltan, which is critical for the production of cellphones and other electronic devices. Conflicts like these not only cost lives but also hinder the development and stability of the regions involved.

Competition over access to natural resources can also pose challenges to environmental sustainability. In the pursuit of resources, companies and governments may engage in unsustainable practices such as overexploitation, deforestation, and pollution. As a result, wildlife habitats are destroyed, ecosystems are disrupted, and biodiversity is diminished, contributing to global environmental degradation.

Furthermore, competition for access to natural resources can exacerbate socioeconomic inequalities. In resource-rich nations, the benefits of resource extraction often do not trickle down to the wider population. Instead, the profits are concentrated in the hands of a few, leading to wealth disparities and social tensions. This, in turn, can foster corruption and political instability, further undermining the development and well-being of communities.

Efforts to address competition over access to natural resources must be multifaceted and inclusive. It requires international cooperation, as well as national policies that prioritize sustainable resource management and equitable distribution. Additionally, measures to promote transparency and accountability in resource extraction can help prevent corruption and ensure that the benefits are shared among the population.

In conclusion, competition over access to natural resources is a complex and multifaceted issue with far-reaching consequences. It affects countries, communities, and the environment on multiple levels. Addressing this competition requires a holistic approach that considers social, economic, and environmental factors, as well as the involvement of all relevant stakeholders. Only through cooperative and sustainable management of resources can we hope to alleviate the pressures and conflicts caused by this competition, ensuring a more equitable and environmentally sustainable future.

3.3 Impacts on International Relations and Diplomacy

The advent of globalization and the rapid advancement of technology have had significant impacts on international relations and diplomacy. These changes have transformed the way nations interact with each other and conduct diplomacy, leading to both positive and negative consequences.

One of the major impacts of globalization on international relations is the increased interdependence among nations. As economies become more interconnected, countries have become highly reliant on each other for trade, investment, and resources. This interdependence has led to a shift in power dynamics, with emerging economies gaining more influence on the global stage. This, in turn, has altered traditional notions of national sovereignty and has required nations to collaborate more closely on global issues such as climate change, public health, and security.

Technological advancements have also had a profound impact on international relations and diplomacy. The rise of digital communication tools and social media platforms has revolutionized the way nations engage with one another. Diplomats can now communicate instantaneously across boundaries, enabling swift decision-making and coordination. This opens up opportunities for increased dialogue and mutual understanding between countries, allowing for more effective resolution of conflicts and better coordination on global issues.

Furthermore, the spread of digital media has also made information more accessible to citizens around the world. This has increased transparency and accountability, forcing governments to be more responsive to public demands. The ability of citizens to share information and mobilize through social media platforms has also empowered civil society organizations to play a more significant role in shaping international agendas.

However, globalization and technological advancements also pose challenges for international relations and diplomacy. The increased interconnectedness of economies has exposed nations to financial vulnerabilities, as seen during the 2008 global financial crisis. Economic shocks in one country can quickly spread across the globe, impacting international trade and increasing political tensions.

Moreover, the rapid spread of information through social media has also created new risks. Misinformation and disinformation campaigns can easily manipulate public opinion and fuel conflicts. Cyberattacks and digital surveillance have also emerged as significant concerns, threatening national security and diplomatic relations. Nations must now navigate the complex landscape of cyber warfare and develop new frameworks and norms to ensure the security and stability of the digital realm.

Furthermore, globalization has led to economic disparities and political inequalities between nations, which can strain diplomatic relations. Developed countries often have more resources and influence to shape international agendas, leading to accusations of neo-colonialism and inequality in decision-making processes. Developing countries may struggle to have their voices heard and their interests represented, leading to challenges in diplomacy and cooperation.

In conclusion, the impacts of globalization and technological advancements on international relations and diplomacy are far-reaching. While they have facilitated increased collaboration, dialogue, and transparency between nations, they have also brought about new challenges and risks. Navigating this rapidly changing landscape requires continued efforts to establish new frameworks and norms that ensure fairness, cooperation, and security in an interconnected world.

Chapter 4: Regional Conflicts and Climate Change

In recent years, the world has witnessed a growing concern over climate change and its potential consequences. The issue has garnered attention not only from environmental activists and scientists but also from policymakers and global leaders. While climate change is a global phenomenon, it has regional implications that may exacerbate existing conflicts or give rise to new ones. This chapter explores the complex relationship between regional conflicts and climate change, shedding light on how a changing climate can contribute to regional tensions.

1. Water Scarcity:

One of the most significant challenges posed by climate change is water scarcity. As global temperatures rise and rainfall patterns shift, many regions are experiencing prolonged periods of drought. The lack of access to freshwater resources has the potential to escalate conflicts over water rights, as demonstrated by the long-standing dispute over the Nile River between Egypt, Sudan, and Ethiopia. In some cases, the competition for water resources may even lead to violence, as seen in conflicts over shared rivers in South Asia and the Middle East.

2. Food Security:

Climate change also poses a threat to food security, particularly in vulnerable regions heavily dependent on agriculture. Rising temperatures, changing rainfall patterns, and increased incidences of extreme weather events such as droughts and floods can lead to crop failures and livestock losses. This, in turn, can trigger food shortages and price volatility, potentially fueling regional conflicts. The situation in Sub-Saharan Africa is particularly dire, where conflicts in countries such as Ethiopia, Somalia, and South Sudan have been linked to a deadly combination of climate change-induced food insecurity and competition over scarce resources.

3. Displacement and Migration:

As the impacts of climate change become more evident, communities living in vulnerable regions are increasingly forced to leave their homes in search of more hospitable environments. Climate-induced displacement and migration put immense pressure on host regions, leading to resource competitions, social tensions, and even violent conflicts. The 2011 Syrian civil war offers a potent example of how a severe drought, exacerbated by climate change, played a significant role in mass displacement and turmoil. As extreme weather events become more frequent and the conditions for agriculture and livelihoods deteriorate, we can expect to see a rise in climate-related displacement, potentially triggering regional conflicts.

4. Natural Resource Competition:

Climate change can intensify competition over natural resources, further exacerbating regional conflicts. As melting Arctic ice opens up new shipping routes and access to previously unreachable oil and gas reserves, states are increasingly vying for control over these resources, leading to heightened geopolitical tensions. Additionally, the race for energy security in the face of declining fossil fuel reserves and the urgency to transition to renewable energy sources can lead to resource-based conflicts. The South China Sea dispute, for example, is driven not only by geopolitical concerns but also by competition over untapped offshore oil and gas reserves.

5. Security Implications:

The interbetween climate change and regional conflicts also introduces significant security implications. Climate-induced conflicts can destabilize entire regions, providing fertile grounds for the rise of extremist ideologies and non-state actors. Moreover, climate change can amplify existing conflicts, making peace processes even more challenging to achieve. For instance, the ongoing conflict in Darfur, Sudan, has been deeply intertwined with climate change-induced resource scarcity, perpetuating violence and hindering attempts at a peaceful resolution.

UNRAVELING THE STORM: A CHAOTIC DANCE OF CLIMATE AND CONFLICT

WHILE THE RELATIONSHIP between regional conflicts and climate change is complex, it is clear that a changing climate has far-reaching implications beyond environmental concerns alone. Water scarcity, food security, displacement, resource competition, and security challenges demonstrate the interconnectedness between climate change and regional conflicts. By understanding these dynamics, policymakers and global leaders can better address and mitigate the potential conflicts arising from a warming planet, emphasizing collaboration, resource management, and sustainable development for a more secure future.

4.1 Climate Vulnerability and Conflict in Africa

Climate change is undeniably one of the most pressing challenges being faced by the global community today. Its far-reaching impacts are being felt across every region, but its consequences are particularly severe in Africa, a continent that is highly vulnerable to climate change.

Africa is known for its diverse climatic conditions, with different regions experiencing varying levels of rainfall and temperature. However, climate change has disrupted these natural patterns, leading to increased frequency and intensity of extreme weather events such as droughts, floods, and storms. These climate-related disasters have had extensive implications for African communities, contributing to food insecurity, water scarcity, and economic destabilization.

The threat posed by climate change is aggravated by the existing socio-economic challenges faced by many African nations. Limited access to healthcare, education, and basic infrastructure, combined with high population growth rates, poverty, and political instability, make African countries more susceptible to the impacts of climate change.

In recent years, there has been growing evidence suggesting a correlation between climate change and conflicts in Africa. The competition over scarce resources such as water and arable land, exacerbated by climate-induced events, has increased existing tensions between different ethnic groups and communities. This resource-induced conflict has resulted in violence, displacement, and loss of life, further intensifying the vulnerability of already marginalized populations.

For example, the ongoing conflict in the Sahel region of Africa, which spans across countries like Burkina Faso, Mali, and Niger, has been greatly fueled by climatic factors. Droughts and desertification have rendered large areas of farming land unproductive, leading to economic hardship and food insecurity. The resulting tensions between nomadic herders and sedentary farmers have escalated into violent clashes, which have been exploited by extremist groups seeking to expand their influence.

Similarly, in the Horn of Africa, the El Niño-induced drought in 2011 contributed to political unrest and violence in Somalia. The collapse of agriculture and livestock, combined with the influx of climate-induced refugees, put a strain on already fragile governance structures, leading to increased conflict and the emergence of extremist groups.

Addressing the climate vulnerability-conflict nexus in Africa requires a comprehensive and coordinated effort from the international community. Investments need to be made to enhance resilience and adaptive capacity of African nations. This includes strengthening early warning systems, improving water resource management, promoting sustainable agriculture and land use practices, and facilitating access to clean energy. Additionally, efforts should be made to promote dialogue and cooperation between different ethnic communities to prevent resource-induced conflicts.

Furthermore, it is necessary to support African countries in their efforts to mitigate greenhouse gas emissions and transition to low-carbon development pathways. This will require financial and technological assistance from developed nations, as well as the commitment to honor global climate commitments, such as those outlined in the Paris Agreement.

In conclusion, Africa faces immense challenges in dealing with the impacts of climate change. The vulnerabilities experienced by African nations are not only environmental but are intertwined with complex socio-economic, political, and cultural factors. Understanding the climate vulnerability-conflict nexus is crucial for developing effective strategies to address the root causes of conflict and build resilience in Africa. By investing in both adaptation and mitigation measures, the international community can assist African nations in their quest for sustainable development and a more secure future.

4.2 Asia-Pacific: Rising Tensions over Disputed Resources

Asia-Pacific: Rising Tensions over Disputed Resources

The Asia-Pacific region has seen rising tensions in recent years as countries compete over disputed resources. From oil and natural gas to fish stocks and rare earth minerals, these resources are seen as crucial for economic growth and national security.

One of the main areas of contention is the South China Sea, where multiple countries have competing territorial claims. China, Vietnam, Malaysia, Taiwan, Brunei, and the Philippines all assert their sovereignty over various islands and reefs in the region. These disputed waters are rich in oil and natural gas deposits, making them highly coveted.

China has been particularly assertive in asserting its claims in the South China Sea, constructing artificial islands and military installations in contested areas. This has raised alarm bells among its neighbors and led to increased tensions. The United States, which has a strong interest in maintaining freedom of navigation in the region, has also voiced its concern over China's actions.

Another source of tension in the region is the dispute between Japan and China over the East China Sea. Both countries claim sovereignty over the Senkaku/Diaoyu Islands, a group of uninhabited islets. The area is believed to have significant oil and gas reserves, adding to the strategic importance of the islands.

In addition to energy resources, the Asia-Pacific region is also home to rich fishing grounds. Overfishing and illegal fishing practices have led to depleting fish stocks, which in turn have fueled confrontations between countries. The contested waters of the South China Sea, for example, are one of the world's most prolific fisheries. As such, competition over fishing rights has become another flashpoint for disputes in the region.

Rare earth minerals, a group of seventeen elements critical to the production of technology products, have also become a subject of rivalry. China currently dominates the global rare earth market, accounting for the majority of production and processing. This has caused concerns among other countries, as dependence on China for these essential minerals raises questions of supply chain security and geopolitical influence.

The rise of tensions over disputed resources in the Asia-Pacific region has important implications for regional stability and global politics. Conflicts over energy resources and fishing grounds have the potential to escalate into military confrontations, affecting not only the countries directly involved but also their allies and partners. Additionally, control over critical minerals could give countries a significant advantage in terms of technological development and economic competitiveness.

Efforts have been made to address these disputes through diplomatic means, such as negotiations and arbitration. However, finding a mutually acceptable resolution is no easy task, given the complexity of the issues involved and the deeply entrenched interests of the countries concerned. As such, the future of these resource disputes in the Asia-Pacific remains uncertain.

In conclusion, rising tensions over disputed resources in the Asia-Pacific region pose challenges to regional stability and global security. Whether it is the South China Sea, the East China Sea, or the competition over fishing grounds and rare earth minerals, these disputes have the potential to spark conflicts and reshape the geopolitical landscape. Finding peaceful and sustainable solutions to these resource disputes is essential to maintaining peace and prosperity in the region.

4.3 Arctic Disputes in the Age of Global Warming

Arctic disputes have gained significant attention in recent years due to the effects of global warming. The melting of Arctic ice has opened up new possibilities for resource extraction, shipping routes, and scientific exploration. As a result, several nations have taken an interest in claiming sovereignty over parts of the Arctic region, leading to ongoing disputes and complex legal implications.

One of the main reasons behind these disputes is the potential for vast natural resource reserves in the Arctic. It is estimated that the region holds substantial deposits of oil, natural gas, and minerals. As the ice continues to melt, accessing these resources becomes more feasible and economically enticing. This has led nations like Russia, Canada, Denmark, Norway, and the United States to stake their claims over specific areas, often overlapping in some cases.

Russia, in particular, has become increasingly assertive in securing its interests in the Arctic. The country has been investing heavily in infrastructure development, military capabilities, and scientific research in the region. In 2001, Russia submitted a claim to the United Nations, asserting that the Lomonosov Ridge, an underwater mountain range spanning the Arctic, is an extension of its continental shelf. This claim would potentially grant Russia control over a significant portion of the Arctic, including the North Pole.

Canada also has its own claims in the Arctic, as it considers the Northwest Passage to be part of its inland waters. This assertion is disputed by other countries, especially the United States, who view the Northwest Passage as an international strait. The issue of the Northwest Passage's legal status has important implications for shipping routes, as the melting ice has made the passage increasingly navigable. Melting ice also opens the possibility for new trade routes between Asia and Europe, providing a more direct and efficient path than through the Panama Canal.

Denmark has also entered the dispute over Arctic territory by asserting sovereignty over Greenland. Being an autonomous territory of Denmark, Greenland strengthens Denmark's position in any Arctic negotiations. Additionally, Norway has its own interests in the Arctic due to its desire to expand its oil and gas exploration activities northwards.

The United States has been more cautious in its approach to the Arctic disputes. Although it has not made explicit claims in the region, the United States sees itself as a major stakeholder, considering Alaska's geographical proximity to the Arctic. The U.S. position is more focused on international cooperation, as it emphasizes the peaceful resolution of conflicts, freedom of navigation, and adherence to international law.

Throughout all the disputes and conflicting claims, the impacts of global warming on the Arctic remain of utmost concern. The region is witnessing unprecedented changes, including shrinking ice cover, rising temperatures, and environmental degradation. The loss of ice poses a threat to wildlife habitats, exacerbating climate change, and potentially leading to geopolitical tension over resources.

In light of these challenges, there have been various efforts to address Arctic disputes on multiple levels. The United Nations Convention on the Law of the Sea (UNCLOS) plays a key role in regulating territorial claims and defining how land and maritime boundaries are determined. The eight Arctic countries have also formed the Arctic Council, a cooperative forum to discuss common issues such as environmental protection, indigenous rights, and scientific research.

The age of global warming has undoubtedly complicated Arctic disputes, with economic, geopolitical, and environmental factors all contributing to the complexity. As the Arctic continues to open up, the need for international cooperation and dialogue becomes paramount in ensuring the sustainable development and preservation of this unique and fragile region.

Chapter 5: Conflict over Climate Adaptation

Climate change is a worldwide phenomenon that has prompted a pressing need for communities and governments to adapt to its impacts. However, the process of climate adaptation is not without its fair share of challenges and conflicts. In this chapter, we delve into the complexities surrounding climate adaptation and explore the various conflicts that arise in its pursuit.

1. The Need for Climate Adaptation:

At its core, climate adaptation is the process of adjusting to the changing climate conditions in order to minimize vulnerability and capitalize on potential opportunities. Rising temperatures, extreme weather events, and sea-level rise are just a few examples of the climate change impacts that necessitate adaptation. Efforts in climate adaptation aim to ensure the resilience of ecosystems, economies, and communities.

2. The Politics of Adaptation:

Climate adaptation is inherently political as it involves decision-making, resource allocation, and redistribution of burdens and benefits. When it comes to shaping adaptation policies and measures, conflicts often emerge between different stakeholders, including government bodies, businesses, NGOs, and local communities. These conflicts stem from divergent priorities, limited resources, and power dynamics.

3. Equity and Justice:

One of the persistent areas of conflict in relation to climate adaptation revolves around issues of equity and justice. Climate change impacts are not distributed equally across regions or populations, and certain groups, such as marginalized communities, may bear a disproportionate burden of the negative consequences. Conflicts arise when it comes to deciding on the allocation of resources and determining who should be responsible for tackling adaptation challenges.

4. Competing Interests:

Another source of conflict in climate adaptation arises from competing interests. Businesses and industries might oppose certain adaptation measures if they perceive them as a threat to their profits or operations. Agricultural communities could clash with conservationists over the use of land for climate adaptation projects. Conflicts can also arise between urban and rural areas in terms of resource distribution and prioritization.

5. Scientific Uncertainty:

Uncertainty surrounding climate change impacts and the effectiveness of particular adaptation measures can also spark conflicts. As scientific knowledge evolves, disagreements may arise about the best course of action or the urgency of implementing certain measures. Decision-makers must navigate divergent scientific opinions, which can heighten conflicts and hinder climate adaptation progress.

6. Governance and Institutional Challenges:

Effective climate adaptation requires robust governance structures and coordination across multiple sectors and scales. However, conflicting mandates, competing regulatory frameworks, and inadequate institutional capacity can impede progress. Moreover, governance mechanisms may fail to adequately engage local communities in decision-making processes, leading to conflicts between top-down and bottom-up approaches.

7. Financial Constraints:

A significant challenge within climate adaptation efforts is the availability and allocation of resources. Developing and implementing adaptive measures often requires substantial financial investment. Conflicts can emerge when decision-makers must address the question of resource distribution among competing priorities, such as education, healthcare, and economic development. Disputes may also arise over who should bear the financial burdens of adaptation, with conflicts arising between developed and developing nations.

CONFLICT IS AN INHERENT part of the climate adaptation process due to the complexity, competing interests, and uncertainties involved. Recognizing and addressing these conflicts is essential for successful adaptation efforts. Adequate governance structures, inclusive decision-making processes, resource availability, and equity considerations are key elements in mitigating conflict and maximizing the effectiveness of adaptation initiatives.

5.1 Challenges in Allocating Climate Funds

Allocating climate funds is a critical aspect of addressing the challenges posed by climate change. These funds play a crucial role in supporting mitigation and adaptation efforts, helping countries transition towards greener economies, reducing greenhouse gas emissions, and building resilience against the impacts of climate change. However, the process of allocating climate funds is not without its challenges. In this article, we will explore some of the 5.1 challenges that come with allocating climate funds.

One of the most significant challenges in allocating climate funds is the sheer complexity of the task. Climate finance involves a wide array of actors, such as governments, multilateral organizations, private institutions, nonprofit organizations, and communities. Coordinating and aligning the efforts of these diverse stakeholders is not an easy undertaking. The funds must be channeled effectively to ensure that they reach the right places and are utilized efficiently. Monitoring how funds are spent and evaluating their impact can also become a cumbersome process.

Another challenge is the unequal distribution of climate funds across regions and countries. The most vulnerable nations, which often contribute little to global greenhouse gas emissions, are also the ones experiencing the most severe impacts of climate change. These countries require substantial financial resources to adapt to climate change and implement mitigation measures. However, they often face difficulties in accessing adequate funds due to issues like limited institutional capacity, bureaucratic hurdles, and lack of appealing investment projects. Closing this financing gap and creating a fair and equitable distribution of funds remains a significant challenge.

Additionally, the unpredictable nature of climate finance poses its challenges. The amount of funding allocated for climate change projects fluctuates from year to year, making it challenging for countries to plan their long-term climate strategies. This unpredictability creates uncertainty for governments, making it difficult for them to commit to long-term projects or policies that require sustained financial support.

Transparency and accountability are also challenges that need to be overcome in the allocation of climate funds. With the influx of climate finance, the risk of corruption and mismanagement increases. Ensuring that funds are used appropriately and effectively is crucial to maintain public trust and maximize the impact of climate finance. Robust monitoring and reporting mechanisms, as well as strong governance structures, are necessary to address these challenges and ensure transparency and accountability in the allocation process.

Finally, the long-term financing of climate change projects is a persistent challenge. Climate change is a global problem that requires long-term and sustained financial commitment. Many climate projects take years to implement, and support needs to be continuous to achieve meaningful impact. However, climate funding often comes in small, short-term projects, creating gaps in funding and hindering the implementation of long-term projects.

In conclusion, allocating climate funds is a complex and challenging task. The distribution of funds must be fair and equitable, accounting for the unique needs of vulnerable countries. Transparency, accountability, and long-term financing are also crucial considerations. While these challenges may seem daunting, addressing them is essential to drive effective climate action and ensure a sustainable future for all.

5.2 Resilience and Conflict Mitigation Strategies

Resilience and conflict mitigation strategies are essential tools in managing and addressing conflicts within any organization. These strategies promote effective communication, collaboration, and problem-solving, enabling individuals and teams to navigate conflicts and challenges successfully.

One major aspect of building resilience and fostering conflict mitigation within teams and organizations is the development of emotional intelligence. Emotional intelligence refers to the ability to understand, manage, and express emotions effectively. It helps individuals recognize and empathize with others' emotions, promoting a more open and understanding environment. By embracing emotional intelligence, teams can find common ground, work towards consensus, and prevent conflicts from escalating.

Another key component of resilience and conflict mitigation is creating an open and inclusive culture that respects diversity. This includes actively seeking diverse perspectives, listening to all team members' voices, and valuing their unique contributions. By understanding and appreciating different viewpoints, teams can build stronger relationships and avoid conflicts due to misunderstandings or biases.

Effective communication is also crucial for building resilience and mitigating conflicts. Open and transparent communication helps prevent misunderstandings, build trust, and address concerns promptly. Encouraging active listening and facilitating constructive conversations can help resolve conflicts and minimize potential negative outcomes. Teams should also establish appropriate communication channels and forums to ensure all key information is shared and discussed effectively.

Conflict resolution and problem-solving techniques are at the core of any conflict mitigation strategy. Effective strategies can involve addressing conflicts head-on, facilitating mediation processes, or utilizing team-building exercises to enhance understanding and collaboration. Encouraging solution-oriented thinking and focusing on mutual gain can also have a positive impact on conflict mitigation and resilience.

Furthermore, building resilience involves recognizing and learning from past challenges and conflicts. This includes conducting thorough evaluations and root cause analyses to understand the underlying issues that may have led to conflicts. By addressing these root causes, steps can be taken to prevent similar conflicts in the future and promote resilience within the organization.

Regular training and development programs can enhance team members' skills in conflict management and resilience building. These programs can provide individuals with tools and techniques to effectively address conflicts, manage stress, and bounce back from setbacks. Offering opportunities for personal growth and professional development can further enhance resilience within the organization, ensuring continuous improvement and adaptability in the face of adversity.

In summary, resilience and conflict mitigation strategies play a vital role in managing conflicts within organizations. By fostering emotional intelligence, developing inclusive cultures, promoting effective communication, and utilizing appropriate conflict resolution techniques, teams and organizations can navigate conflicts and challenges successfully. Investing in training and learning opportunities can also enhance individuals' skills and contribute to long-term resilience within the organization.

5.3 Inequities in Climate Adaptation Efforts

In this section, we will delve into the topic of inequities in climate adaptation efforts. Climate change is an issue that affects everyone, but unfortunately, not everyone is impacted equally. Certain groups, especially those already marginalized, face greater challenges in adapting to the changing climate. This creates an inequitable distribution of resources and support, exacerbating social and economic inequalities.

One of the main reasons for these inequities is the uneven distribution of resources. Communities that are already economically disadvantaged have fewer resources available to invest in climate adaptation efforts. This lack of financial means restricts their ability to implement measures such as building climate-resilient infrastructure, improving agricultural practices, or investing in clean energy solutions. As a result, these communities are more vulnerable to the adverse impacts of climate change, including extreme weather events, food insecurity, and water scarcity.

Moreover, marginalized groups often face additional barriers when it comes to accessing support and resources. Discrimination, exclusion, and power imbalances can limit their participation in decision-making processes and prevent them from voicing their concerns and needs regarding climate adaptation. This lack of representation can result in adaptation strategies that fail to adequately address the specific challenges faced by these groups, further perpetuating inequality.

Education and awareness also play a significant role in determining the effectiveness of climate adaptation efforts. In many cases, marginalized communities lack the necessary knowledge and information about climate change and its impacts. This can hinder their ability to adapt and make informed decisions about how to protect themselves and their livelihoods. Access to accurate and relevant information, along with educational programs, is crucial in empowering communities to respond effectively to climate change.

Additionally, the geographic location of certain populations can make them more susceptible to climate-related risks. For example, low-income communities of color living in coastal areas are disproportionately affected by sea-level rise and increased flooding. Their livelihoods, homes, and infrastructure are at higher risk, and relocation might not be a viable option due to financial constraints or lack of available resources. This creates a cycle of inequality, as these communities continue to face compounded risks without the means to adapt.

Efforts to address these inequities require a multi-faceted approach. Governments and international organizations need to prioritize climate justice and ensure that resources and funding are distributed equitably. Investments should be made in strengthening the capacity of marginalized communities to adapt, including providing financial resources, technical support, and capacity-building programs.

Furthermore, inclusivity and stakeholder engagement should be prioritized in decision-making processes. Engaging with and including marginalized groups in policy discussions and adaptation planning is vital in ensuring that their concerns and needs are taken into account. This inclusivity can also contribute to more innovative and effective adaptation strategies that benefit the entire community.

Education and awareness campaigns targeted towards marginalized communities are essential. These programs should provide accessible information about climate change, its impacts, and adaptive measures that individuals and communities can take. By arming these groups with knowledge and empowering them to participate in decision-making processes, their adaptive capacity can be enhanced.

In conclusion, inequities in climate adaptation efforts create a disproportionate burden on marginalized communities. Lack of resources, limited access to support, and a lack of awareness all contribute to this disparity. Addressing these inequities requires a comprehensive approach that includes equitable distribution of resources, inclusivity in decision-making processes, and targeted educational programs. By doing so, we can work towards achieving climate justice and ensure that the burdens and benefits of adaptation are shared more fairly.

Chapter 6: Climate-Induced Security Risks

Climate change is not only a threat to our environment and natural resources but also has the potential to undermine global security. The intricate relationship between climate change and security is increasingly gaining attention in academic, political, and policy-making circles. This chapter delves into climate-induced security risks, discussing their complexity, impact, and potential consequences.

Climate Change and Security Nexus:

The complexities of climate-induced security risks can be understood by examining the interconnectivity between climate change and political, economic, and societal factors. The adverse effects of climate change, such as extreme weather events, sea-level rise, and water scarcity, can act as catalysts for various security threats. These threats include resource competition, mass migration, territorial disputes, conflict escalation, and instability in already fragile regions.

Impact on Resource Competition:

Climate change can exacerbate competition over limited resources, leading to tension and conflicts. With shrinking glaciers, changing rainfall patterns, and increased drought frequency, access to water resources has become a critical issue. The competition for water is likely to intensify, especially in regions where freshwater is already scarce. Similarly, degraded land and limited agricultural productivity can lead to competition for fertile soil, exacerbating food insecurity and creating ethnic tensions.

Mass Migration and Refugees:

Climate change-induced environmental degradation can cause large-scale displacement of people, often leading to refugee crises. Rising sea levels threaten low-lying areas and small island states, forcing people to migrate in search of safer areas. Additionally, extreme weather events and their aftermath, such as hurricanes or floods, can render regions uninhabitable. Mass migrations driven by climate change can strain infrastructure, increase the risk of social unrest, and place immense pressure on host communities.

Territorial Disputes:

The impact of climate change on territorial boundaries and maritime zones adds another layer of complexity to security risks. As sea levels rise, coastal territories may vanish, triggering conflicts over territorial claims, exclusive economic zones, and access to valuable marine resources. Furthermore, disputes may escalate as countries compete over new trade routes becoming accessible due to melting Arctic ice. Such tensions can escalate to conflicts and further destabilize geopolitically sensitive regions.

Conflict Escalation and Instability:

Climate-induced security risks can exacerbate existing tensions, fuel rebellions, and prompt conflicts. Scarce resources, shocks to the economy, and displacement can breed social unrest and contribute to political and societal instability. Communities that rely heavily on agriculture and subsistence farming are particularly vulnerable to these climate-induced dynamics. Moreover, extreme events like droughts or cyclonic storms can tip the balance and destabilize even relatively stable environments.

Consequences and Global Implications:

The implications of climate-induced security risks are not limited to specific regions; they have the potential to reverberate globally. Conflict and instability in one region can affect international trade, disrupt supply chains, and force migration flows towards neighboring regions or even across continents. In the age of globalization, the domino effect of climate-induced security risks can have profound implications for international peace and stability.

UNDERSTANDING AND ADDRESSING climate-induced security risks is of paramount importance to global security. It requires an integrated approach involving not only environmental measures but also political, economic, and humanitarian efforts. Creating resilience, fostering cooperation, and developing adaptation strategies can play a crucial role in minimizing the security risks associated with climate change.

While the complexities involved pose significant challenges, it is essential to recognize and act upon the interdependencies between climate change, resource scarcity, mass migrations, territorial disputes, conflict, and global security. By doing so, we can effectively mitigate the potential consequences and build a resilient and stable future for generations to come.

6.1 Extreme Weather Events and Humanitarian Crises

Extreme weather events and humanitarian crises have become an increasingly common occurrence in our rapidly changing world. These events, such as hurricanes, floods, droughts, and heatwaves, have severe impacts on both human populations and the environment.

One of the primary causes of extreme weather events is climate change. As greenhouse gases accumulate in the atmosphere, temperatures rise, leading to more frequent and intense weather phenomena. This increased frequency and intensity of extreme weather events pose significant challenges to communities and societies worldwide, particularly those in vulnerable regions.

Hurricanes, for example, are becoming more powerful due to rising ocean temperatures. The increased intensity of these storms results in stronger winds, storm surges, and flooding, causing widespread destruction of infrastructure, loss of homes, and even loss of life. The 2017 Atlantic hurricane season, which saw hurricanes Harvey, Irma, and Maria, was a stark reminder of the devastating impacts these events can have. They crippled entire islands, disrupted critical transport and communication networks, and left communities without access to basic necessities.

Similarly, floods are increasingly common and severe in many regions. As precipitation patterns shift due to climate change, certain areas may experience heavier rainfall, leading to a greater risk of flooding. These flood events also pose health risks by contaminating water sources and spreading waterborne diseases. In 2010, devastating floods hit Pakistan, affecting over 20 million people and causing significant damage to infrastructure, agriculture, and livelihoods.

Another example of the effects of extreme weather events is droughts. Rising temperatures can lead to increased evaporation rates, drying out soils and water sources, and significantly reducing available water supplies. Droughts have devastating consequences on agriculture and food security, triggering crop failures, livestock deaths, and hunger. Sub-Saharan Africa has experienced severe droughts in recent years, resulting in widespread food shortages and humanitarian crises.

Additionally, heatwaves are becoming more frequent and intense globally. High temperatures can lead to extreme heat stress, impacting human health, agriculture, water resources, and energy production. The heatwave in Europe in 2003 caused tens of thousands of excessive deaths and resulted in significant economic losses. The 2019 heatwave in India also claimed many lives and affected agricultural production.

Humanitarian responses to these extreme weather events are crucial in reducing their impacts and saving lives. Aid organizations and national governments must work together to develop robust disaster preparedness and response strategies. This includes providing early-warning systems, effective evacuation plans, ensuring access to clean water and sanitation, and delivering medical aid and relief supplies to affected communities.

Efforts should also focus on minimizing the environmental impacts that exacerbate these extreme weather events. Reducing greenhouse gas emissions and promoting sustainable practices can help mitigate climate change and lessen the frequency and intensity of such events in the long term.

Furthermore, strategies for building resilience in vulnerable communities must be implemented. This includes investing in infrastructure that can withstand extreme weather conditions, diversifying livelihoods to reduce dependence on climate-vulnerable sectors, and improving access to education and resources to empower communities to respond effectively to crises.

In conclusion, extreme weather events and humanitarian crises are interlinked, complex challenges requiring urgent action. The effects of climate change are amplifying these events, posing significant risks to human populations and the environment. Effective responses that encompass disaster preparedness, mitigation, and resilience-building strategies are essential to reducing the impacts of extreme weather events and ensuring sustainable development in the face of a changing climate.

6.2 Militarization of Climate Action

The topic of militarization of climate action is a complex and multifaceted one. It involves examining the various ways in which the military is involved in addressing climate change, both as a response to the changing climate and as a contributor to it. In this section, we will delve into the details of this issue, exploring its implications and the arguments surrounding its merits and drawbacks.

One aspect of militarization of climate action is the military's role in responding to the impacts of climate change. As extreme weather events become more frequent and intense, the military is often called upon to provide support in disaster relief and humanitarian assistance. This could include providing emergency supplies, rescuing stranded individuals, and assisting in rebuilding efforts. The military's resources and logistical capabilities make it well-equipped to respond quickly and effectively in times of crisis.

However, critics argue that relying on the military for climate response places too much focus on the symptoms rather than addressing the root causes of climate change. By diverting resources towards disaster response, governments may be neglecting the importance of mitigation and adaptation efforts. Additionally, militarization can come with a heavy cost, both in financial terms and in terms of long-term security implications. It has been reported that significant amounts of military funding are being allocated to climate-related activities, at the expense of other vital needs such as healthcare and education. This raises concerns about whether these funds would be better invested in sustainable development and renewable energy solutions that address the underlying causes of climate change.

A notable example of militarization of climate action is the role of the military in energy security. Fossil fuel resources have historically been a major driver of geopolitics and conflict, and as the world transitions towards renewable energy sources, the military plays a key role in securing access to these resources. This can manifest in various ways, such as military interventions in oil-rich regions and the protection of critical energy infrastructure. However, this can also perpetuate a cycle of resource exploitation and exacerbate the very climate threats we are trying to address. The reliance on fossil fuels for military operations is also a significant contributor to greenhouse gas emissions, with the military being one of the largest consumers of fossil fuels globally. Therefore, some argue that the military should focus on reducing its own carbon footprint before engaging in climate action efforts.

Another aspect of militarization of climate action is the emerging field of climate security. This involves studying the potential security risks and conflicts arising from climate change, such as water scarcity, displacement, and food insecurity. The military, with its expertise in analyzing and managing risks, is increasingly involved in these discussions. Some argue that this is a necessary and valuable contribution, as climate change is expected to amplify existing conflicts and create new security threats. By integrating climate considerations into military planning and risk assessments, governments can better prepare for and mitigate these risks. However, critics warn that securitizing climate change may overshadow the urgent need for global cooperation and collective action. They argue that a militarized response may prioritize national security over international cooperation, hindering collaborative efforts to address the shared threat of climate change at a global scale.

In conclusion, the militarization of climate action is a complex and controversial topic that merits careful consideration. While the military's capabilities and expertise can be valuable in responding to climate-related challenges, it is important to ensure that efforts are not solely focused on symptoms and short-term solutions. Long-term sustainable solutions, including the reduction of military greenhouse gas emissions and the transition towards renewable energy, should be prioritized. At the same time, securitizing climate change must not overshadow the need for international cooperation and collective action. Balancing the goals of climate action and security will undoubtedly require a comprehensive and multidimensional approach.

59

6.3 Implications for Global Peacekeeping Efforts

Global peacekeeping efforts are essential for maintaining international stability and preventing conflicts from escalating into full-scale wars. In recent years, multiple factors have surfaced that directly impact the success and effectiveness of these peacekeeping operations. This article will delve into the implications of these factors and their consequences for global peacekeeping efforts.

Firstly, the rise of non-state actors and terrorist organizations has posed a significant challenge for peacekeeping operations worldwide. These groups operate across borders and engage in unconventional warfare tactics, targeting civilians and infrastructure. Their presence and activities undermine fragile peace agreements and hinder the implementation of peacekeeping missions. UN peacekeepers often find themselves dealing with these groups in complex and unfamiliar situations, forcing them to adopt unconventional strategies while adhering to peacekeeping principles. As a result, global peacekeeping efforts require a significant shift in focus and approach to effectively counter these emerging threats.

Secondly, the proliferation of modern technology and social media platforms has drastically altered the way conflicts unfold and the methods employed by parties involved. Innovative communication technologies have allowed both state and non-state actors to disseminate propaganda, recruit members, and coordinate attacks on a global scale. Peacekeeping missions must adapt and stay abreast of these advancements to effectively intercept these activities. The proficient incorporation of technology into peacekeeping efforts is crucial for keeping pace with these new challenges.

UNRAVELING THE STORM: A CHAOTIC DANCE OF CLIMATE AND CONFLICT

Moreover, the swift diffusion of information through these technological platforms has also led to increased international scrutiny of peacekeeping operations. In the past, peacekeepers operated in relative obscurity, their actions only known to a few. However, in today's interconnected world, the global public demands transparency and accountability from peacekeepers. Instances of misconduct by peacekeeping personnel or missions can tarnish the reputation and impartiality of these operations, potentially undermining public trust and support. Therefore, global peacekeeping efforts need to prioritize ethical conduct and robust oversight mechanisms to maintain credibility and legitimacy.

Additionally, environmental degradation and resource scarcity have emerged as significant factors contributing to global conflicts and security challenges. Climate change-induced resource scarcity, such as water and arable land, can exacerbate existing tensions and cause communal disputes. Peacekeeping missions should thus adopt an integrated approach by considering the environmental aspects of peace and security. This means addressing the root causes of conflicts while taking into account the sustainable use of resources and promoting environmental resilience.

Furthermore, the ever-increasing complexities of conflicts require peacekeepers to possess an extensive range of skills and expertise. As conflicts become more asymmetrical and multifaceted, peacekeeping forces need to be adequately trained in handling a wide range of scenarios, such as civilian protection, nation-building, and human rights promotion. Developing countries that contribute troops to peacekeeping missions often require support to enhance their capacities and capabilities, from logistical and financial assistance to training and knowledge sharing. Ensuring well-prepared and adequately equipped peacekeepers is imperative to effectively carry out global peacekeeping efforts.

Finally, the evolving nature of peacekeeping mandates contributes to the implications for global peacekeeping efforts. Previously, peacekeeping missions focused primarily on traditional interstate conflicts, monitoring ceasefires, and supervising peace agreements. However, contemporary peacekeeping mandates often involve complex tasks, such as facilitating political transitions, supporting post-conflict reconstruction, and protecting civilians during ongoing conflicts.

These expanded mandates require empowering peacekeepers with the necessary tools, resources, and authority to carry out their responsibilities effectively.

In conclusion, the implications for global peacekeeping efforts are far-reaching and multifaceted. The rise of non-state actors, advancements in technology, demands for transparency, environmental challenges, and evolving mandates all contribute to the changing landscape of global peacekeeping. Addressing these implications requires adaptability, innovation, and a collaborative approach. Only through an understanding of these implications and the implementation of effective strategies can global peacekeeping efforts hope to nurture a more peaceful and stable world.

Chapter 7: Conflict-Driven Environmental Destruction

Conflict has been an unfortunate reality throughout human history, with its devastating consequences reverberating across societies and the environment. When conflicts arise, natural resources often become strategic targets, leading to widespread environmental destruction. This chapter explores the complex relationship between conflict and the environment, focusing on how conflicts exacerbate environmental degradation and the subsequent feedback loop that can perpetuate violence. It also sheds light on examples from different parts of the world where conflict-driven environmental destruction has had severe and long-lasting impacts.

1. Conflict and Natural Resources:

Natural resources are essential for human well-being and economic development. However, they often become a source of contention and rivalry during conflicts. This is because valuable resources, such as oil, minerals, timber, and water, can provide substantial financial incentives, fuelling the conflict and creating a vicious cycle of violence and environmental degradation. Armed groups and militias may exploit natural resources to fund their activities, leading to overexploitation, pollution, and irreparable damage to ecosystems.

1.1. Resource War:

The concept of a "resource war" emerges when conflicts are primarily fought over scarce resources, such as water or territory with valuable resources. The quest for control or ownership of these resources can intensify conflicts, triggering violence that further exacerbates environmental destruction. This phenomenon has been witnessed in various regions, with examples like the Darfur conflict in Sudan, where scarce water resources led to competition, displacement, and ultimately amplifying tensions.

1.2. Resource Curse:

The Resource Curse theory explains how countries rich in natural resources often experience setbacks in development, social stability, and environmental preservation. It suggests that the presence of abundant resources can create corruption, inequality, and a lack of institutional mechanisms to protect the environment. Oil-rich states, such as Nigeria or Venezuela, illustrate how conflicts and environmental devastation are intertwined, as disputes over resource revenues inflame violence and hinder sustainability efforts.

2. Environmental Consequences of Conflict:

Conflict significantly impacts the environment, culminating in dire and long-lasting consequences for ecosystems, biodiversity, natural resources, and human health. The extensive use of weaponry, such as landmines or heavy artillery, leads to soil contamination and habitat destruction. War-related activities like deforestation for military purposes or expanding refugee camps contribute to habitat fragmentation and biodiversity loss, disrupting delicate ecological balances.

2.1. Water Scarcity:

In many conflict zones, water becomes a coveted and scarce resource. Destruction of vital water infrastructure, contamination from chemical spills or untreated waste, and population displacement lead to water scarcity, risking public health and exacerbating social tensions. Moreover, competition over water resources and hydroelectric projects can fuel political unrest, as seen in the the Nile water dispute and geopolitical rivalries in the Middle East.

2.2. Pollution and Toxic Waste:

Weapons, particularly modern ones, often involve the use of hazardous substances that pose significant risks to the environment. Explosives, heavy metals, and toxic chemicals contaminate soil, water bodies, and air, poisoning both ecological systems and vulnerable populations. The long-term consequences include reduced agricultural productivity, disease outbreaks, and higher cancer rates in affected areas.

3. Feedback Loop: Conflict-driven environmental destruction perpetuating violence:

Conflict-driven environmental destruction not only impacts the environment but also perpetuates the cycle of violence. As natural resources diminish, competition escalates, intensifying the conflict and making it more enduring. Moreover, environmental hardships caused by warfare, such as loss of livelihoods or food insecurity, further exacerbate grievances among affected populations, making them vulnerable to recruitment by armed groups.

3.1 Conflict and Illegal Resource Exploitation:

Armed groups often exploit areas beset by conflict to engage in lucrative illegal activities like resource extraction, logging, or wildlife trafficking. Illegal trade networks, driven by the demand for conflict minerals, such as coltan or diamonds, and endangered species products, fund armed conflicts, subvert governance, and exacerbate environmental destruction. Broader international cooperation and enforcement are necessary to disrupt these illicit flows and break the cycle of violence associated with such activities.

3.2. The Role of Natural Resource Governance:

Improving natural resource governance is crucial in preventing conflict-driven environmental destruction. Effective and transparent management of natural resources requires robust legal frameworks, accountable institutions, and inclusive decision-making processes involving local communities. Implementing sustainable practices, such as promoting responsible mining and restoring degraded lands, can help mitigate the destructive impact of conflicts on the environment.

CHAPTER 7 EXPLORES the interconnectedness between conflict and environmental destruction, demonstrating how conflicts can turn valuable resources into instruments of violence and war. The resulting environmental degradation not only harms ecosystems and biodiversity but also perpetuates the cycle of violence, making conflict resolution and sustainable development more challenging. Understanding this complex interaction is crucial for developing strategies that address conflict-driven environmental destruction and foster peacebuilding efforts rooted in sustainable environmental management.

7.1 Deforestation and increased Forest Fires

Deforestation refers to the permanent destruction of forests to meet various human needs such as agriculture, logging, urbanization, and infrastructure development. Over the past few decades, deforestation has become a significant environmental concern, with severe consequences for biodiversity, climate change, and natural resource availability. One of the most alarming impacts of deforestation is the increased frequency and intensity of forest fires.

As forests are cleared for agricultural purposes, the vegetation that acts as a natural firebreak is removed, leaving the area susceptible to wildfires. Additionally, the dense canopy cover in forests helps to retain moisture, creating a more humid environment that is less prone to fires. However, with deforestation, this natural protection is lost, and the newly exposed dry land becomes highly susceptible to catching fire.

Moreover, logging activities contribute to deforestation and the potential for forest fires. Logging leaves behind logging debris, which forms flammable accumulations on the forest floor, providing ample fuel for fires to spread quickly. This logging debris, known as slash, dries out quickly and can easily ignite due to the high temperatures in deforested areas. Once a fire is ignited within these logging debris-filled areas, it can rapidly escalate into large-scale forest fires due to the presence of extensive amounts of fuel.

Deforestation also disrupts the hydrological cycle, leading to drier conditions which further enhance the risk of forest fires. Trees play a crucial role in absorbing and retaining moisture from rainfall. When forests are cut down, the transpiration process is reduced, resulting in reduced humidity in the surrounding area. This decrease in humidity combined with the accumulation of dried vegetation sets the stage for the outbreak and rapid spread of fires.

Climate change is another factor that contributes to the increased frequency of forest fires following deforestation. Global warming leads to rising temperatures, prolonged droughts, and altered precipitation patterns, all of which create favorable conditions for wildfires. The combination of deforestation and climate change results in a vicious cycle, wherein deforestation contributes to climate change, which in turn fuels the intensity and frequency of forest fires.

The ecological impact of increased forest fires is profound. Forests are home to a diverse range of plant and animal species, many of which are unable to escape fire-prone areas. These forest fires destroy habitats, disrupt ecosystems, and often lead to the loss of unique species. The loss of forests also hampers the planet's ability to absorb carbon dioxide, exacerbating climate change even further.

Addressing deforestation and its connection to the increased incidence of forest fires is crucial for the preservation of our planet. Strong policies to protect and preserve forests, along with sustainable land use practices, need to be implemented. Building awareness about the impacts of deforestation and promoting reforestation initiatives are also vital steps in combating this pressing issue.

In conclusion, deforestation is a complex and far-reaching problem with numerous environmental consequences. Increased forest fires are a direct consequence of deforestation, posing threats to biodiversity, climate change, and the well-being of communities residing near forests. Recognizing the importance of forests, implementing sustainable practices, and advocating for policy changes are necessary steps in mitigating the effects of deforestation on forest fires and safeguarding a sustainable future for our planet.

7.2 Damages to Ecosystems and Biodiversity

Damages to ecosystems and biodiversity have become a pressing issue in the modern world. Human activities have had a profound impact on the natural environment, often resulting in irreversible damage to ecosystems and the loss of biodiversity. This article will delve into the intricate details of how damages occur and explore the fascinating consequences of such actions.

One of the primary causes of damages to ecosystems and biodiversity is habitat destruction. As human populations continue to grow, the need for land intensifies. This desire for land, whether for agriculture, urbanization, or industrial purposes, often comes at the expense of natural habitats. Forests are cleared, wetlands are drained, and grasslands are converted for human use. This destruction of natural habitats disrupts the delicate balance of ecosystems, leading to the displacement of numerous plant and animal species. Many animals rely on specific habitats for their survival, and when these habitats are destroyed, their survival is compromised, leading to their decline or even extinction.

Another significant source of damages to ecosystems is pollution. Pollution can take many forms, including air, water, and soil pollution. Whether it's the release of toxic gases into the atmosphere from industrial activities or the dumping of hazardous chemicals into rivers and lakes, pollution has detrimental effects on ecosystems and biodiversity. Pollution can lead to the death of plant and animal life, contaminate food chains, and disrupt habitats. Additionally, pollution has wider environmental impacts, contributing to climate change, which further exacerbates damages to ecosystems and biodiversity.

Invasive species also pose a threat to ecosystems and biodiversity. When non-native species are introduced into new environments, they can outcompete native species for resources, disrupt food chains, and alter entire ecosystems. Invasive species often lack natural predators, allowing their populations to grow unchecked. This can result in the root cause of the unique local biodiversity being replaced by a handful of dominant, non-native species. The consequences of introduced invasive species can be highly detrimental to the overall health and resilience of ecosystems.

Climate change is yet another factor responsible for damages to ecosystems and biodiversity. The rise in global temperatures caused by human activities, such as the burning of fossil fuels, has far-reaching effects on ecosystems. Rising temperatures lead to changes in precipitation patterns, altering the availability of water and causing immense stress to ecosystems. For example, coral bleaching, a result of warmer water temperatures, is devastating coral reefs worldwide. The loss of coral reefs has a knock-on effect throughout the ecosystem, impacting the numerous species that rely on reefs for their survival.

The fragmentation of ecosystems is also a cause for concern. Increased infrastructure development, such as roads and urban areas, can fragment habitats, isolating populations and inhibiting genetic exchange between individuals. This fragmentation reduces the resilience of ecosystems and makes it harder for species to adapt to changing environmental conditions. The consequences of habitat fragmentation can include reduced genetic diversity, increased vulnerability to diseases, and reduced availability of resources.

The damages to ecosystems and biodiversity discussed above have numerous far-reaching consequences. One of the most significant consequences is the loss of essential ecosystem services that ecosystems provide. Ecosystem services, such as pollination, water purification, and carbon sequestration, are crucial for human well-being. Without the proper functioning of ecosystems, these services can decline, negatively affecting human societies. Additionally, the loss of biodiversity can disrupt the stability of ecosystems, making them more susceptible to disturbances and less able to recover from them.

Addressing damages to ecosystems and biodiversity requires a multi-faceted approach. It is essential to prioritize sustainable land use practices that minimize habitat destruction and ensure the preservation of natural habitats. Reducing pollution through regulatory measures and transitioning to cleaner energy sources is also crucial. Additionally, efforts must be made to prevent the introduction and spread of invasive species and to promote measures that mitigate the impacts of climate change. Finally, maintaining the connectivity of ecosystems through the protection of wildlife corridors and the reduction of fragmentation is vital for promoting biodiversity conservation.

In conclusion, the damages inflicted on ecosystems and biodiversity are of great concern. The causes of these damages encompass habitat destruction, pollution, invasive species, climate change, and habitat fragmentation. The consequences of these damages are far-reaching, affecting ecosystem services and the stability of ecosystems. To address these issues effectively, a multi-faceted approach is needed that prioritizes sustainable land use practices, pollution reduction, invasive species management, climate change mitigation, and the promotion of connectivity between habitats. Only through collective efforts can we strive to repair and restore the damages caused to ecosystems and biodiversity.

7.3 Clashes over Land Use and Resource Extraction

Clashes over land use and resource extraction have been a persistent and contentious issue throughout history. From ancient times to the present day, communities and governments have clashed over the rights and ownership of land, as well as the extraction and utilization of valuable resources.

One of the main reasons for these clashes is the inherent value that land and resources hold. Throughout history, land has been seen as a source of wealth, power, and livelihoods. From fertile soils for agriculture to mineral-rich territories for mining, land has been a coveted asset for individuals, communities, and nations alike.

However, the perceived value of land and resources often leads to conflicts when different stakeholders have diverging interests. Indigenous communities, for example, have frequently struggled to protect their ancestral lands from encroaching settlements, agriculture, or resource extraction projects. The clash between the rights of indigenous peoples and the desires of governments or corporations for access to natural resources has been a recurring theme globally.

In many cases, clashes over land use and resource extraction go beyond issues of ownership and economic interests. Environmental concerns often come into play, as the exploitation of natural resources can have severe consequences for ecosystems and the people who depend on them. Deforestation, for instance, can lead to habitat destruction, loss of biodiversity, and increased vulnerabilities to natural disasters.

Furthermore, clashes over land use and resource extraction often exacerbate existing social inequalities, especially in countries with weak governance institutions and rampant corruption. Miners, loggers, and other extractive industries are notorious for working conditions that exploit workers and endanger their lives. These industries are also frequently linked with environmental degradation and pollution, which disproportionately affect marginalized communities living near extraction sites.

In recent years, clashes over land use and resource extraction have become increasingly complex and intense due to global challenges such as climate change and population growth. As the demand for resources continues to rise, governments and corporations face pressure to find new ways to meet this demand. This often involves expanding into territories that were previously inaccessible or deemed ecologically sensitive.

The issue of land grabs has also become a prominent concern. Large-scale land acquisitions by foreign investors, often in developing countries, have triggered conflicts with local communities who depend on the land for their livelihoods. These acquisitions, commonly known as land grabs, have displaced communities and disrupted traditional ways of life, leading to increased poverty and social unrest.

Addressing clashes over land use and resource extraction requires a multi-faceted approach. It requires a balance between economic growth and environmental sustainability, as well as protecting the rights and livelihoods of indigenous communities and vulnerable groups. Governments need to work towards transparent and inclusive decision-making processes that involve local populations, allowing them to have a say in how their land and resources are used.

The international community also has a role to play in ensuring responsible practices by companies operating in foreign countries. Strong regulations, agreements, and sanctions can help prevent exploitative resource extraction practices and ensure that the benefits of resource exploitation are distributed more equitably.

In conclusion, clashes over land use and resource extraction are complex and multifaceted issues that require careful management and consideration. Balancing the economic, social, and environmental aspects of land and resource utilization is crucial to ensuring a sustainable and equitable future for all.

Chapter 8: Climate Induced Terrorism

Climate change has become an existential crisis for humanity, impacting various facets of our lives. However, one less explored aspect is the potential acceleration of terrorism due to climate-induced conditions. This chapter aims to delve into the intricate relationship between climate change and terrorism, particularly focusing on the emergence of "climate-induced terrorism" as a rising threat. By examining the historical context, underlying factors, and potential future scenarios, we seek to shed light on a relatively uncharted territory of security concerns.

1. Historical Context:

The link between climate change and security threats is not a recent discovery. Historically, resource scarcity, agricultural downturns, and environmental disruptions have often intensified conflicts and fueled insurgencies. However, as the impacts of climate change amplify, these factors are projected to worsen, leading to an increase in the occurrence and severity of terrorism.

2. The Nexus between Climate Change and Terrorism:

Climate change will lead to a series of multi-faceted socio-economic and political consequences, resulting in fertile ground for extremist ideologies and radicalization. Below are some key factors:

a. Resource Scarcity: Climatic changes, such as water scarcity and declining agricultural productivity, can trigger the competition for limited resources. This can ignite conflicts and propel vulnerable populations towards extremist ideologies as a means of survival.

b. Climate Refugees: As climate change displaces millions from their homes due to rising sea levels, extreme weather events, or deteriorating agricultural conditions, massive movements of people are expected. These refugees risk becoming vulnerable to radicalization, recruitment by terrorist groups, or even becoming agents of terror themselves.

c. Collapse of Governance: Climate change-induced effects on governance can lead to state fragility and even collapse. The resulting power vacuum can enable terrorist organizations to exploit instability and establish safe havens, further exacerbating the security threat.

d. Economic Disruptions: Climate change-driven disturbances, such as food shortages, economic recessions, and decreased livelihood opportunities, disproportionately impact already marginalized communities. These economic insecurities, combined with limited access to basic necessities, can contribute to the resorting of certain individuals towards acts of terrorism as a perceived pathway to redemption or justice.

3. Recent Examples of Climate-induced Terrorism:

a. Boko Haram: In the Sahel region of Africa, prolonged drought and desertification have caused widespread food shortages, poverty, and displacement. Boko Haram, seeking to exploit the grievances of the affected populations, has capitalized on these conditions to recruit fighters and sustain its operations.

b. Al-Shabaab: Somalia's prolonged droughts and subsequent famine have been major catalysts for radicalization and the recruitment of new members into Al-Shabaab, an extremist group infamous for its terrorist activities.

4. Future Scenarios and Policy Implications:

The projected scenarios of climate change paint a grim picture of its interwith terrorism. Policy makers and security organizations need to recognize the imminent security implications and take proactive measures:

a. Early Warning Systems: Development and implementation of early warning systems, capable of detecting societal tensions arising from climate-induced vulnerabilities, can allow for proactive intervention and conflict resolution.

b. Climate Change Adaptation Measures: Incorporating climate change adaptation strategies into national security plans can be instrumental in countering the exacerbation of terrorism through climate-induced conditions.

c. International Cooperation: Collaboration among nations to address the root causes of climate change, invest in sustainable development, and enforce mitigation measures can significantly reduce the potential for climate-induced terrorism.

THE NEXUS BETWEEN CLIMATE change and terrorism presents an emerging security challenge that necessitates attention and action. By understanding the complex interplay between these two seemingly distinct phenomena, policymakers, security experts, and communities can collectively strive to safeguard against the intensified threats that climate-induced terrorism poses. As climate change continues to shape our global landscape, addressing these issues becomes imperative for long-term security and stability worldwide.

8.1 Rising Extremism due to Climate Change

Climate change is undoubtedly one of the most pressing challenges of our time. Its far-reaching impacts are already being felt around the globe, with devastating consequences for both human beings and the natural world. However, there is another dangerous consequence of climate change that often goes unnoticed- rising extremism.

As climate change worsens, it exacerbates existing social, economic, and political inequalities. This gives rise to a sense of despair and desperation among many communities that are particularly vulnerable to the impacts of climate change, such as marginalized populations and developing countries. These groups often bear the brunt of extreme weather events, food and water shortages, and displacement, leaving them in a state of perpetual precarity.

In this environment, extremist ideologies find fertile ground to take root and grow. Extremist groups, be it fringe political movements or radical religious organizations, capitalize on the fear and uncertainty triggered by the consequences of climate change. They offer simplistic narratives and convenient scapegoats to explain the complex and multifaceted challenges that communities face. This engenders a sense of belonging and purpose among their members, as they seemingly address their followers' concerns and fears.

The spread of extremist ideologies due to climate change manifests in various ways. In certain regions affected by environmental degradation and resource scarcity, extremist groups exploit people's frustrations by providing them with an alternative guiding principle- one that champions division, hostility, and violence rather than cooperation, compassion, and peace. In this climate, it becomes much easier to recruit disenchanted individuals who feel abandoned by their governments and abandoned by the international community to their cause.

Additionally, there is evidence that climate change-induced conflicts and climate-related disasters lead to social displacement and forced migration. Large-scale movements of people, whether within national borders or across them, create opportunities for extremist groups to infiltrate and exploit vulnerable populations. Displaced individuals, seeking safety and stability, may be drawn to extremist ideologies while living in crowded, resource-scarce environments that lack adequate infrastructure and support systems. This further contributes to the growth of extreme ideologies driven by climate change.

Moreover, climate change can also foster extremism by intensifying existing geopolitical tensions. Competing interests over dwindling resources, particularly in areas experiencing increased desertification or water scarcity, can lead to confrontations between nations. Such conflicts often rekindle dormant ethnic or religious grievances, making them even more volatile. In this context, extremist groups seize the opportunity to fuel strife and exploit divisions to further their own agendas.

To effectively counter rising extremism due to climate change, a holistic approach is required. Governments and international institutions must prioritize addressing the root causes of extremism, including social and economic disparities. Investing in education, providing job opportunities, and ensuring access to basic services can help create a sense of stability and security that lessens the appeal of extremist ideologies.

Moreover, collaboration and cooperation between nations are crucial to mitigate the impacts of climate change and reduce the vulnerability of communities. By working together to develop sustainable and resilience-building strategies, the international community can create a safer and more equitable world that resists the encroachment of extremist ideologies.

Ultimately, it is incumbent upon all individuals to recognize the link between climate change and rising extremism. By educating ourselves and raising awareness about the ways in which climate change can contribute to societal upheaval, we can start having informed conversations and take concerted action to address this complex issue. Only by tackling both the immediate consequences and underlying causes of climate change can we hope to prevent the further spread of extremism and build a brighter, more secure tomorrow.

8.2 Role of Climate Change in Recruitment and Radicalization

Climate change has long been recognized as a global issue with wide-ranging and far-reaching impacts on the environment, economy, and society. However, recent research suggests that climate change may also play a significant role in the recruitment and radicalization of individuals towards extremist ideologies.

One of the key ways in which climate change affects recruitment and radicalization is through its impact on vulnerable populations. The changing climate can lead to increased poverty, food and water scarcity, and displacement of communities. These challenges create fertile ground for extremist groups to exploit the grievances of marginalized individuals and offer them a sense of purpose and belonging. As people struggle to survive and find their basic needs met, radical ideologies can provide a seemingly attractive alternative to their current desperate situation.

A study conducted by researchers at Stanford University found that crop failures driven by climate change can contribute to an increase in civil unrest and violence. The study analyzed data from Africa and Asia and found a strong correlation between droughts and the likelihood of armed conflict. As resources become scarce, competition over land, water, and food can escalate into violence, providing extremist groups with a recruiting ground for disenchanted and disillusioned individuals.

Moreover, climate-induced displacement and migration can also contribute to the recruitment of individuals into extremist organizations. Displaced people often find themselves in overcrowded camps or informal settlements with little to no support or opportunity for a better life. This lack of security and hope can make them vulnerable to radicalization as extremist groups prey on their frustrations and promise a better future, greater justice, and revenge against perceived oppressors.

The spread of misinformation and conspiracy theories about climate change and its causes also fuels radicalization. Some extremist groups, particularly those with an anti-government or anti-establishment stance, seek to exploit fears and uncertainty surrounding climate change to rally followers to their cause. By spreading false narratives about climate science, they create a sense of distrust towards authorities and the mainstream, legitimate efforts to address environmental challenges. This can result in vulnerable individuals falling victim to these propaganda campaigns and becoming radicalized.

Furthermore, climate change can exacerbate existing ethnic and religious tensions, leading to an increased likelihood of radicalization. In regions already marked by social, political, or religious strife, environmental stressors can intensify these conflicts and provide an added impetus for extremist ideologies to emerge. The limited availability of diminishing resources in times of ecological crisis can deepen societal divisions and exacerbate grievances, making it easier for extremist groups to manipulate and recruit individuals along the lines of identity or ideology.

Addressing climate change and its impact on the recruitment and radicalization process requires a multifaceted and integrated approach. It is essential to mitigate the causes and effects of climate change, including reducing greenhouse gas emissions and promoting sustainable development. Additionally, efforts must be made to address the socio-economic factors that contribute to vulnerability and reduce the likelihood of radicalization. This involves strengthening social safety nets, promoting inclusive governance, and ensuring equitable access to resources and opportunities.

Lastly, countering extremist propaganda and promoting fact-based information about climate change is crucial. Engaging communities through education and awareness campaigns can help build resilience against radical ideologies and foster critical thinking skills necessary to distinguish between reliable scientific information and misinformation.

In conclusion, the role of climate change in recruitment and radicalization is a complex and emerging issue. By exacerbating inequality, social grievances, and resource scarcity, climate change provides fertile ground for extremist ideologies to flourish. Addressing this connection requires comprehensive action to mitigate climate change, strengthen social resilience, and promote inclusive societies. Combating misinformation and promoting fact-based understanding will also play a crucial role in preventing the further radicalization of vulnerable individuals.

Chapter 9: Migration and Conflict

Migration has been a fascinating and complex phenomenon throughout the history of humanity. It is driven by various factors such as economic, political, social, and environmental. However, migration is not always free from conflicts. In fact, migration itself can often create conflicts, both between host communities and migrants, as well as among the migrants themselves. This chapter aims to explore the relationship between migration and conflict and provide an in-depth understanding of this dynamic interaction.

Migration and Conflict: A Historical Perspective

Migration has been historically linked to conflicts, for different reasons and in various forms. Many ancient civilizations experienced conflicts resulting from the movement of people. The invasion and conquest of territories by migrating populations were often driven by conflict and the clash of different cultures. For example, the fall of the Roman Empire was largely influenced by the invasion of migrating barbarian tribes.

Economic Factors: A Cause and Consequence of Conflict

Economic factors play a crucial role in migration-related conflicts. Migrants often leave their home countries in search of better economic opportunities, which can create tensions in host communities. Natives may perceive migrants as a threat, fearing competition for jobs and resources. This fear can escalate into conflicts, leading to discrimination, xenophobia, and even violence.

Moreover, economic disparities between migrants and locals can create inequality, which further exacerbates the potential for conflicts. Exploitation of migrant labor, low wages, and poor working conditions can breed resentment and eventually result in social unrest or strike actions.

UNRAVELING THE STORM: A CHAOTIC DANCE OF CLIMATE AND CONFLICT

Political Factors: Power Struggles and Ethnic Tensions

Political factors also contribute significantly to migration-related conflicts. In many instances, migration flows are driven by political unrest, persecution, or conflicts in the migrants' home countries. Such large-scale movements can disrupt existing power dynamics and create ethnic tensions. For example, the Yugoslav Wars in the 1990s gave rise to a massive wave of refugees who fled towards neighboring countries, resulting in conflicts over shared resources and ethnic rivalries.

Furthermore, the political manipulation of migration for ideological or electoral purposes can also create conflicts. Politicians often exploit anti-immigrant sentiments to gain support by fueling fear and resentment towards migrants. This manipulation not only perpetuates conflict but also hinders efforts to foster integration and peaceful coexistence.

Social Factors: Cultural Clashes and Social Exclusion

Migration can bring about cultural clashes between migrants and the host communities, leading to social tensions and conflicts. Values, traditions, norms, and beliefs may differ significantly, causing misunderstandings and animosities. Social exclusion, stemming from cultural differences and prejudice, can marginalize migrants and limit their access to basic rights and services. This exclusion, in turn, fosters conflicts and undermines social cohesion.

Conflict Among Migrants: Merging Identities and Competition

Conflict is not limited to interactions between migrants and host communities. Rivalries and clashes frequently arise amongst the migrants themselves. Migration introduces diverse groups with distinct ethnic, cultural, and social backgrounds, which can result in competition for resources and recognition. Such competition can escalate into conflicts, reflecting power struggles and the redefining of collective identities within migrant communities.

Conflict Resolution: Promoting Integration and Peaceful Coexistence

Addressing the conflicts that arise from migration requires a holistic approach. It entails fostering social integration, combating discrimination, promoting economic development, and guaranteeing legal protection for migrants. Promoting intercultural dialogue, creating platforms for grievances to be addressed, and enhancing cooperation between communities are vital steps towards peaceful coexistence.

Additionally, international cooperation is crucial in managing migration-related conflicts. Collaborative efforts among nations, organizations, and local communities can help address the underlying causes of conflicts, manage the impact of migration, and promote mutual understanding and respect.

MIGRATION AND CONFLICT are deeply intertwined, with migration often being a flashpoint for disputes and tension. Understanding the complexity and interplay of various factors that contribute to migration-related conflicts is essential to developing effective solutions. By addressing the economic, political, and social aspects that underlie these conflicts, and promoting integration and peaceful coexistence, we can strive towards a more harmonious coexistence between migrants and host communities.

9.1 Implications of Climate Migration on Host Communities

Climate migration refers to the movement of people due to the impacts of climate change on their homes. As climate change continues to exacerbate extreme weather events, sea-level rise, and other environmental disruptions, it is estimated that millions of individuals will be displaced and forced to seek new homes in the coming decades. This phenomenon has far-reaching implications not only for those who are migrating but also for the host communities that receive them.

One of the most significant implications of climate migration on host communities is the strain it places on existing resources and infrastructure. Climate migrants often seek shelter, food, water, and other basic necessities upon arriving in a new place. This sudden influx of people can overwhelm local governments and services, leading to overcrowding, increased demand for social services, and resource shortages. Host communities may struggle to accommodate the needs of both their existing citizens and the new arrivals.

Another challenge faced by host communities is the socio-economic impact of climate migration. Many climate migrants are forced to leave behind their homes, assets, and livelihoods, and often lack the financial resources to rebuild their lives in a new location. This can result in the formation of informal settlements or slums as migrants struggle to find housing and employment opportunities. These informal settlements may lack access to basic services such as healthcare, education, and sanitation, posing challenges to public health and exacerbating inequality within host communities.

In addition to the strain on resources and socio-economic challenges, climate migration can also have cultural and social implications. Host communities may experience a cultural clash as they are confronted with an influx of individuals from different backgrounds and ethnicities. This can lead to tensions, discrimination, and xenophobia, especially if local communities perceive the migrants as a burden or a threat to their way of life. Effective integration and dialogue between migrants and host communities are crucial to ensure the development of inclusive and harmonious societies.

It is also essential to recognize the positive potential of climate migration on host communities. Migrants often bring with them unique skills, knowledge, and cultural diversity, contributing to the social and economic fabric of their new homes. They can revitalize local economies, fill labor gaps, and enhance cultural exchange. However, realizing these benefits requires proactive policies and frameworks that support the integration and inclusion of migrants.

In conclusion, climate migration presents significant implications for host communities. It strains existing resources and infrastructure, poses socio-economic challenges, and can lead to cultural tensions. However, with thoughtful planning, cooperation, and inclusive policies, these challenges can be addressed, and the potential benefits of climate migration can be harnessed to create stronger and more resilient communities.

9.2 Border Security and Migration Laws in a Warming World

Border Security and Migration Laws in a Warming World: Balancing Interests in a Complex Challenge

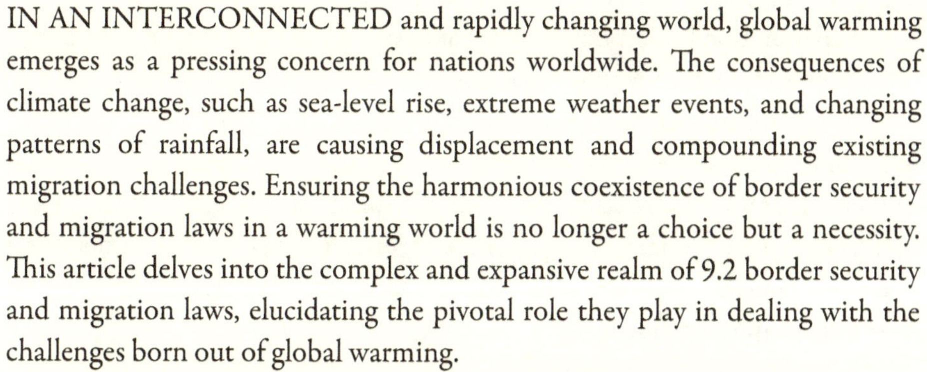

IN AN INTERCONNECTED and rapidly changing world, global warming emerges as a pressing concern for nations worldwide. The consequences of climate change, such as sea-level rise, extreme weather events, and changing patterns of rainfall, are causing displacement and compounding existing migration challenges. Ensuring the harmonious coexistence of border security and migration laws in a warming world is no longer a choice but a necessity. This article delves into the complex and expansive realm of 9.2 border security and migration laws, elucidating the pivotal role they play in dealing with the challenges born out of global warming.

1. Understanding the Impact of Climate Change on Migration:

Rising temperatures and environmental degradation prompt population movements, provoking both internal and cross-border migration. Severe droughts, dwindling agricultural productivity, and increasingly inhospitable territories force vulnerable communities to abandon their homes in search of safer, more sustainable livelihoods. Such climate-induced displacement places enormous strains on border security frameworks worldwide.

2. The Delicate Balance between Security and Protection:

Border security policies encompass an intricate dance between securing national borders while simultaneously offering protection to individuals fleeing the negative consequences of climate change. Striking the right balance between these opposing interests is challenging, as nations need to adopt empathetic and forward-thinking approaches that align with the principles of human rights and international refugee law.

3. Addressing Migrants as Climate Refugees:

One way to harmonize migration laws and border security in a warming world is by recognizing climate-induced migrants as climate refugees. This acknowledgment would allow for international assistance while providing these individuals with legal avenues for entry and support upon resettlement. It requires a paradigm shift in recognizing climate as a genuine basis for claiming asylum.

4. Regional Approaches and Cooperation:

The complexities associated with climate change require comprehensive regional frameworks to address shared challenges. Forming alliances, developing joint adaptation strategies, and fostering regional cooperation in managing migration flows can ensure a collective response with mutual benefit. Such collaboration bolsters security without compromising human rights.

5. Environmental Security Measures:

Navigating the impacts of climate change on migration extends beyond managing displaced persons. Environmental security measures play a crucial role in mitigating the root causes of climate-induced migration. Investments in infrastructure, water management systems, and sustainable agricultural practices alleviate pressure on border security by improving resource distribution and livelihoods.

6. Leveraging Technology:

Rapid advancements in technology allow border security agencies to better manage migration flows while safeguarding against potential risks. Smart sensors, data analytics, and biometric systems enhance screening procedures, facilitate efficient processing, and aid in identifying genuine climate refugees. Intelligently utilized technology can augment security and streamline migration processes simultaneously.

7. Empowering Vulnerable Communities:

Comprehensive border security and migration frameworks must also prioritize empowering vulnerable communities to adapt to climate change while recognizing their inherent resilience. Equipping these communities with the necessary knowledge, support, and resources to withstand challenges further enhances collective security efforts.

THE INTERTWINED NATURE of border security and migration laws surfaces as a central challenge amid a warming world. It necessitates a multifaceted approach encompassing legal reforms, regional cooperation, environmental security measures, and technological innovation. Balancing the interests of security and protection while comprehensively addressing climate-induced displacement is not only an ethical obligation but a strategic imperative. By adopting inclusive and forward-thinking practices, nations can establish frameworks that not only ensure border security but also protect and empower those most affected by the rising threat of climate change.

9.3 Conflict Dynamics in Temporary Shelter Settlements

Conflict Dynamics in Temporary Shelter Settlements: Understanding, Analyzing, and Mitigating Challenges

TEMPORARY SHELTER SETTLEMENTS are an essential refuge for displaced populations in times of crisis, offering them security, safety, and vital resources. However, the dynamics within these settlements can be complex and challenging, often leading to conflicts among residents. It is crucial to understand the intricacies of these conflicts, analyze their causes, and devise effective strategies to mitigate them. This article aims to delve into conflict dynamics in temporary shelter settlements, bringing forth relevant and thought-provoking information.

1. Nature of Conflicts:

Conflicts in temporary shelter settlements may arise due to various reasons, including competition for limited resources such as food, water, and healthcare services. Other factors such as cultural differences, power struggles, grievances, and the trauma experienced by individuals can also play a significant role in conflict escalation. Understanding the nature of these conflicts helps in developing targeted interventions.

2. Impact on Residents:

Conflicts adversely affect the physical and psychological well-being of displaced individuals. Due to their vulnerability and traumatic experiences, they may be more susceptible to trauma, anxiety, and depression. Moreover, conflicts often disrupt community cohesion and compromise the provision of essential services, worsening the living conditions in temporary settlements.

3. Role of Infrastructure and Design:

The physical layout and infrastructure of temporary shelter settlements can either perpetuate or alleviate conflicts. Poorly designed, congested spaces with inadequate access to water and sanitation facilities can intensify tensions and contribute to disputes. Conversely, well-planned settlements that prioritize communal spaces, privacy, and access to basic services can provide avenues for conflict resolution and promote social harmony.

4. Importance of Stakeholder Engagement:

Engaging various stakeholders, including residents, humanitarian organizations, local authorities, and host communities is critical to understanding and addressing conflicts within temporary settlements. Incorporating the perspectives of all stakeholders can ensure that conflict resolution strategies are context-specific and sustainable, fostering future resilience within the settlements.

5. Conflict Mitigation Strategies:

To effectively manage conflicts in temporary settlements, the implementation of comprehensive conflict resolution strategies is essential. These may include establishing community-based mediation mechanisms, providing training in conflict resolution and peacebuilding skills, promoting dialogue and mutual understanding, and creating opportunities for income generation and livelihoods. Regular monitoring and evaluation of these initiatives are vital in gauging their effectiveness.

6. Gender Dynamics and Conflict:

Gender dynamics play a pivotal role in temporary shelter settlement conflicts. Gender-based violence, discrimination, and power imbalances can exacerbate conflicts and hinder conflict resolution efforts. It is essential to consider gender perspectives in all conflict mitigation strategies, ensuring the empowerment and inclusion of women and marginalized groups.

TEMPORARY SHELTER SETTLEMENTS serve as vital lifelines for displaced populations, but they also face significant challenges related to

conflict dynamics. By understanding the underlying causes, impacts, and mitigation strategies of conflicts, stakeholders can work collectively to transform these settlements into spaces of safety, resilience, and sustainable communal living. Through strategic interventions and stakeholder engagement, we can pave the way for the creation of prosperous and harmonious temporary shelter settlements.

Chapter 10: Innovative Solutions to Climate Change and Conflict

As the world grapples with the interrelated challenges of climate change and conflict, there is an increasing need for innovative solutions that can address these complex issues. In this chapter, we will explore some of the key innovative approaches that are being employed to simultaneously tackle climate change and conflict, with a focus on their potential impact and effectiveness.

1. Climate-responsive peacebuilding

One innovative solution that has emerged in recent years is the concept of climate-responsive peacebuilding. This approach recognizes the linkages between climate change and conflict and seeks to address them holistically. Climate-responsive peacebuilding initiatives aim to promote peace and stability in climate-affected areas by integrating climate change adaptation and mitigation measures into peacebuilding efforts.

These initiatives recognize that climate change can exacerbate existing tensions and conflicts and can also be a driver of new conflicts. By addressing the root causes of conflict, such as competition over scarce natural resources or unequal access to land, water, and other livelihoods, climate-responsive peacebuilding aims to prevent and mitigate conflicts while also strengthening resilience and adaptive capacity in climate-vulnerable communities.

2. Transformational adaptation

Another innovative approach is the concept of transformational adaptation. This approach moves beyond traditional approaches to adaptation, which often focus on incremental measures to cope with climate impacts, and instead seeks to fundamentally transform systems and communities to be more resilient and adaptable.

Transformational adaptation recognizes that many existing systems and structures, such as water management systems or agricultural practices, may be increasingly incompatible with future climate conditions. By identifying and implementing radical changes to these systems, transformational adaptation aims to create sustainable and resilient solutions that can withstand the impacts of climate change.

3. Climate diplomacy and conflict resolution

Climate change is increasingly being recognized as a threat multiplier that can exacerbate existing conflicts or create new ones. In response, there has been growing recognition of the need for climate diplomacy and conflict resolution mechanisms to address the security implications of climate change.

Innovative approaches to climate diplomacy and conflict resolution include the integration of climate change considerations into peace negotiations and mediation processes. This can involve bringing together stakeholders from different sectors, such as environment, peacebuilding, and development, to facilitate dialogues and find mutually beneficial solutions.

Moreover, innovative technologies, such as satellite imagery and remote sensing, have been utilized to monitor and verify climate-related risks and to support mediation efforts by providing objective data and evidence. Additionally, forward-looking conflict analysis tools and early warning systems using climate data can help identify potential hotspots of climate-related conflicts.

4. Innovative financing mechanisms

Addressing climate change and conflict requires significant financial resources. Innovative financing mechanisms are emerging to mobilize the necessary funding from diverse sources and ensure their efficient allocation.

One such mechanism is the Green Climate Fund, a multilateral fund that channels public and private investments towards climate-resilient projects and mitigation efforts in developing countries. The Green Climate Fund adopts an innovative approach by targeting co-benefits, such as poverty reduction and sustainable development, alongside climate change adaptation and mitigation.

Another example is the concept of climate risk insurance. Climate risk insurance schemes aim to provide vulnerable communities with financial protection against climate-related risks, such as extreme weather events or sea-level rise, thus reducing the potential for conflicts arising from loss and damage.

INNOVATIVE SOLUTIONS to climate change and conflict are crucial as traditional approaches prove inadequate given the scale and complexity of these challenges. The climate-responsive peacebuilding, transformational adaptation, climate diplomacy, and innovative financing mechanisms discussed in this chapter illustrate the potential for creative, integrated solutions to address both climate change and conflict. By embracing these approaches and fostering interdisciplinary collaboration, we can work towards a more secure, equitable, and sustainable future for all.

10.1 Climate Diplomacy and Conflict Resolution

In the realm of global negotiations and conflict resolutions, one area that has gained significant attention and importance is climate diplomacy. As global temperatures continue to rise and the impacts of climate change become increasingly visible, the need for international cooperation becomes even more crucial. The field of climate diplomacy focuses on the interof environmental and foreign policy, aiming to deescalate conflicts and promote sustainable development.

One of the key aspects of climate diplomacy is the recognition that climate change can act as a potential threat multiplier. Climate-related events such as droughts, flooding, and natural disasters can exacerbate existing grievances and tensions within societies, leading to conflicts both between and within countries. These conflicts can range from disputes over water resources to conflicts over land use and migration.

Therefore, the goal of climate diplomacy is not only to address the impacts of climate change but also to prevent conflicts from arising due to the resulting vulnerabilities. Diplomats and negotiators work to promote dialogue and cooperation between nations, encouraging the sharing of resources and technologies that can help mitigate the effects of climate change, thus reducing the potential for conflict.

Furthermore, climate diplomacy also recognizes the importance of addressing social and economic inequalities within and between nations. Many conflicts, both environmental and otherwise, are rooted in these disparities. By promoting sustainable development and facilitating access to resources, climate diplomacy can help establish a foundation for peace and stability.

UNRAVELING THE STORM: A CHAOTIC DANCE OF CLIMATE AND CONFLICT

Understanding the complexities and interconnections between climate change, diplomacy, and conflict resolution requires a multidisciplinary approach. Researchers, policy-makers, and practitioners from various fields, including environmental science, international relations, and peacebuilding, collaborate to develop effective strategies and policies for climate diplomacy.

One example of successful climate diplomacy is the Paris Agreement, adopted in 2015, which aims to limit global warming to well below 2 degrees Celsius above pre-industrial levels. This landmark agreement was achieved through extensive negotiations and cooperation between nations, signaling a global commitment to addressing climate change collectively.

While climate diplomacy has made significant strides in recent years, challenges still remain. Political differences, economic interests, and limited resources can hinder progress and lead to conflicts of interest. Additionally, the urgent need to address climate change requires swift action, prompting debates over the prioritization of short-term versus long-term goals.

Despite these challenges, the importance of climate diplomacy in addressing the impacts of climate change and preventing conflicts cannot be overstated. As the world's population continues to grow, natural resources become scarcer, and the threat of climate change looms, international cooperation and diplomacy are essential to ensure a sustainable future.

In conclusion, climate diplomacy plays a crucial role in conflict resolution by addressing the impacts of climate change, preventing potential conflicts, and promoting sustainable development. The complex and interconnected nature of climate change and diplomacy requires a multidisciplinary approach to develop effective strategies and policies. While challenges persist, climate diplomacy offers hope for a future where environmental and diplomatic solutions intersect, paving the way for a more peaceful and sustainable world.

10.2 Sustainable Development as a Path to International Cooperation

Sustainable development has become a major focus of international cooperation in recent years. With the increasing recognition of the need to protect the environment and promote economic growth in a sustainable manner, governments around the world have come together to work towards common goals through cooperation and collaboration.

One of the key aspects of sustainable development is the recognition that economic growth must be balanced with environmental protection and social progress. In other words, development should be pursued in such a way that it meets the needs of the present without compromising the ability of future generations to meet their own needs. This requires a long-term perspective and the integration of environmental, economic, and social considerations.

International cooperation in the pursuit of sustainable development has several benefits. Firstly, it allows for the sharing of knowledge and best practices across borders. By learning from each other's successes and failures, countries can avoid repeating mistakes and accelerate progress towards sustainable development goals. This knowledge sharing can lead to more effective policies and practices, as governments can draw on the expertise and experiences of others.

Secondly, international cooperation can facilitate the mobilization of resources needed for sustainable development. Many developing countries lack the financial and technological resources necessary to implement sustainable practices on their own. Through international cooperation, these countries can access the funds, technology, and expertise needed to develop and implement sustainable solutions. This can enhance their capacity to achieve their sustainable development goals and promote inclusive and equitable development.

Furthermore, international cooperation can help address global challenges that transcend national boundaries. Issues such as climate change, biodiversity loss, and pollution require collective action and cooperation among countries. Through international agreements and frameworks, countries can coordinate their efforts to address these challenges effectively. For example, the Paris Agreement on climate change aims to limit global warming by building consensus and mobilizing resources at an unprecedented scale.

Last but not least, international cooperation in sustainable development can foster partnerships and build trust among nations. By working together towards a common goal, countries can forge stronger relationships based on shared values and mutual understanding. This can create a conducive environment for cooperation in other areas, improving diplomatic relations and reducing conflicts.

However, international cooperation in sustainable development is not without challenges. One of the key challenges is the differing priorities and interests of countries. While sustainable development is a common goal, countries may have different ideas on how to achieve it or may prioritize other issues over sustainable development. This can hinder cooperation and create tensions among nations.

Another challenge is the uneven distribution of resources and capacities among countries. Some countries may lack the resources or capacity to implement sustainable practices, making them reliant on external support. Bridging this gap and ensuring the equitable distribution of resources and benefits requires concerted efforts from the international community.

In conclusion, sustainable development is a path to international cooperation and holds significant potential for addressing global challenges while promoting inclusive and equitable development. Through international cooperation, countries can share knowledge, mobilize resources, and build partnerships to achieve sustainable development goals. However, it is important to address the challenges associated with differing priorities and uneven distribution of resources to ensure effective international cooperation in sustainable development.

10.3 Climate Change Mitigation as a Means of Conflict Prevention

Climate change has emerged as one of the greatest challenges facing the world today, impacting every aspect of our lives, including politics, economics, and social dynamics. As temperatures rise and extreme weather events become more frequent, the potential for conflicts and instability also increases. In this context, climate change mitigation strategies play a crucial role in preventing conflicts and fostering global stability. This article explores the importance of climate change mitigation as a means of conflict prevention and its potential impact on global security.

1. Climate Change and Conflict:

Climate change is increasingly recognized as a driver of conflicts worldwide. Scarce resources, such as water and fertile land, become increasingly contested as their availability diminishes. Droughts, floods, and reduced agricultural productivity can exacerbate food and water shortages, leading to resource-driven conflicts. Additionally, climate-induced migration can strain host communities and give rise to tensions between different ethnic, religious, or cultural groups. Mitigating the impact of climate change is, therefore, crucial in ensuring stable socio-political environments.

2. Tackling the Root Causes:

Addressing climate change at its root causes is key to preventing conflicts. Mitigation strategies aim to reduce greenhouse gas emissions, halt deforestation, and transition to sustainable energy sources. By mitigating climate change, we can minimize the occurrence of extreme weather events, preserve valuable ecosystems, and provide economic incentives for sustainable development. These measures, in turn, contribute to reducing the likelihood of conflicts driven by resource scarcity and economic inequalities.

3. Renewable Energy Transition:

One of the most impactful mitigation strategies is the transition to renewable energy. Fossil fuel dependency is not only a major contributor to climate change but is also a cause of geopolitical tension, as nations compete for energy resources. By investing in and encouraging the adoption of renewable energy sources, countries can decrease their reliance on fossil fuels, mitigating climate change while potentially defusing long-standing conflicts over energy resources. Moreover, renewable energy projects often require collaboration between countries, promoting cooperation and reducing tensions.

4. Economic Opportunities and Social Stability:

Mitigation efforts offer significant economic opportunities that can contribute to social stability and conflict prevention. Investments in green technologies and clean energy industries can stimulate economic growth and job creation, particularly in developing countries. By diversifying national economies and raising living standards, these opportunities reduce the risk of social unrest and discontent. Additionally, by promoting women's participation in renewable energy initiatives, social inequalities can be addressed, fostering inclusivity and building resilience in marginalized communities.

5. International Cooperation and Diplomacy:

The urgency and magnitude of climate change necessitate international cooperation and diplomacy. Mitigation efforts require collaboration between nations, sharing of technology and expertise, and coordination of policies. Through joint initiatives, countries can build trust, strengthen regional partnerships, and establish mechanisms for peaceful resolution of potential conflicts. Climate change mitigation, therefore, presents an opportunity for diplomacy and collective action, fostering a culture of peace and cooperation on a global scale.

CLIMATE CHANGE MITIGATION represents an essential tool for conflict prevention. By addressing both the direct and indirect consequences of climate change, we can minimize the drivers of conflict and foster global stability. The transition to renewable energy, investments in sustainable development, and international cooperation offer a multi-faceted approach to prevent conflicts caused by resource scarcity, social inequalities, and geopolitical tensions. Urgent and ambitious action is required from all nations to mitigate climate change and secure a peaceful future for all.

Conclusion - Tackling
Climate Change and Conflict

In conclusion, addressing climate change and its relationship with conflict is an urgent task requiring global cooperation and action. This article has shed light on the interconnections between these two pressing issues and highlighted the potential consequences if effective measures are not taken.

Firstly, it has been established that climate change exacerbates existing conflict triggers and creates new ones. Scarce resources, such as water and arable land, often lead to competition and disputes among communities and states. Additionally, extreme weather events can displace people and further strain already vulnerable regions, potentially resulting in heightened hostilities. Understanding the intricate nexus between climate change and conflict is essential to mitigate the impacts effectively.

The analysis provided in this article has also underscored the global nature of climate change and its consequences. No country is immune to its effects, and therefore, international coordination and collaboration are imperative. Global efforts are especially crucial to address climate-induced migration, which can give rise to social tensions and conflicts. By acknowledging that climate change is a shared problem and showing willingness to collaborate, nations can effectively work towards implementing comprehensive solutions and preventive strategies.

Furthermore, the author has highlighted the importance of tackling climate change not merely as an environmental issue but also as a security concern. Recognizing the nexus between the environment, climate, and security is vital in creating policies and frameworks that can be effective in preventing and mitigating conflicts. Integrating these considerations within national security plans is necessary to enhance disaster resilience, manage resource disputes, and prevent future conflicts.

The case studies provided in this article have served to illustrate the various ways in which climate change intersects with conflict. From the Sahel region to Syria, it is evident that environmental degradation and climate-related events have played a significant role in igniting or exacerbating tensions. These real-world examples serve as poignant reminders of the urgent need for action and collaboration.

In response to the challenges posed by climate change and conflict, this article emphasizes the need for a multi-dimensional approach. Such an approach would involve not only mitigation measures to reduce greenhouse gas emissions but also adaptation strategies to enhance resilience in vulnerable regions. International organizations, governments, and civil society must prioritize climate change and conflict on their agendas and allocate resources accordingly.

Finally, this article emphasizes the importance of a bottom-up approach, engaging local communities and stakeholders in decision-making processes. The inclusion of indigenous knowledge and practices can foster sustainable solutions and promote environmental stewardship. Moreover, supporting developing countries in their efforts to adapt and mitigate climate change is essential to ensure global equity and collective responsibility.

In conclusion, this article makes a compelling argument for global action to address climate change and conflict. With its detailed analysis, it offers valuable insights into the complex interplay between these two critical issues. Effective and sustained international cooperation, commitment, and investment are paramount to mitigate climate-related conflicts and cultivate a more peaceful and sustainable world for future generations. It is only through collective action that we can hope to tackle the challenges posed by climate change and safeguard our global security and well-being.

- Tackling Climate Change and Conflict: A Call for Global Action

CLIMATE CHANGE IS UNDENIABLY one of the most pressing challenges humanity faces in the modern era. Its impacts are far-reaching and have the potential to upend societies, disrupt livelihoods, exacerbate existing inequalities, and even fuel conflicts. The intertwined relationship between climate change and conflict is a complex issue that requires urgent attention and collective action from the international community. This article aims to delve into the intricacies of this relationship, highlighting the need for a global approach to address both climate change and the resulting conflicts.

Understanding the Climate-Conflict Nexus:

Climate change and conflict present a feedback loop that perpetuates a vicious cycle of deterioration. On one hand, climate change acts as a threat multiplier, exacerbating existing social and economic vulnerabilities. Rising temperatures, erratic rainfall patterns, sea-level rise, and extreme weather events, among other climate impacts, directly impact livelihoods and disrupt essential resources such as water and food security. These environmental stressors, coupled with limited resources, increase competition and tensions within communities, often leading to conflicts over scarce resources.

On the other hand, conflicts themselves have detrimental effects on the environment. Resource-intensive conflicts, such as those driven by disputes over water, land, or energy, further deplete already stressed ecosystems. Instances of environmental degradation, including deforestation, pollution,

105

and unsustainable resource extraction, can rise in the midst of conflicts where governance is weakened or absent.

Conflict itself also hampers the ability to address climate change effectively. The damage caused by conflicts, whether in physical infrastructure or societal institutions, diverts resources away from mitigation and resilience-building efforts. Furthermore, conflict disrupts long-term planning and collaboration, as immediate security concerns take precedence. This barrier to action perpetuates vulnerability to climate change and intensifies the likelihood of further conflicts in the future.

Case Studies:

Numerous case studies illustrate the complex intersections between climate change and conflict. Take, for example, the ongoing conflict in the Lake Chad region of Africa. Climate change-induced drought, combined with increased population pressure, has led to resource competition, exacerbating tensions between nomadic herders and sedentary farmers. This aggravated violence along ethnic lines further fuel political instability and extremism in the region.

Similarly, in the Middle East, Syrian civil war has been linked to a severe drought from 2006 to 2011, which displaced rural communities and increased economic hardships. These internal tensions eventually spilled over into a full-blown conflict, exacerbating existing geo-political rivalries, and creating a regional quagmire with multifaceted international implications.

The Call for Global Action:

Addressing the climate-conflict nexus necessitates global action from governments, multilateral institutions, civil society, and individuals alike. First and foremost, international cooperation in scaling up climate mitigation and adaptation efforts is vital. Reducing greenhouse gas emissions, investing in renewable energy, and implementing climate-resilient agricultural practices are crucial steps in averting the worst climate impacts and reducing conditions that could trigger conflicts.

Simultaneously, promoting conflict prevention and peace-building measures have a role to play in addressing the climate-conflict nexus. This involves investing in conflict-sensitive programming, inclusive governance structures, and peace diplomacy. Strengthening early warning systems and enhancing social cohesion can help reduce community vulnerabilities and prevent conflicts from exacerbating environmental stressors.

UNRAVELING THE STORM: A CHAOTIC DANCE OF CLIMATE AND CONFLICT

International institutions, such as the United Nations and regional bodies, also have a responsibility to integrate climate change and conflict considerations into their policies and frameworks. The inclusion of climate-security dimensions in peace negotiations and the support of climate adaptation in conflict-affected regions can help address both immediate and long-term challenges.

Moreover, public awareness and education play a crucial role in engaging individuals and communities and fostering a broad-based commitment to tackling the climate-conflict nexus. Empowering grassroots organizations, indigenous communities, and women, who are disproportionately affected by climate change and conflicts, is vital for inclusive action.

IN CONCLUSION, THE urgent need to tackle climate change and mitigate conflicts is undeniably interconnected. The impacts of climate change exacerbate existing social tensions and fuel conflicts, while conflicts diminish the capacity to address climate change, perpetuating a destructive feedback loop. Understanding the climate-conflict nexus and advocating for combined global action is critical in the face of this complex challenge. By addressing the root causes, investing in resilience-building, and promoting peace-building efforts, we can embark on a path towards a more sustainable and peaceful world.